Illinois Central College
Learning Resources Center

THE DOCTRINE OF VIRTUE

Works in Continental Philosophy
GENERAL EDITOR JOHN R. SILBER

IMMANUEL KANT, 1724 - 1804.

The DOCTRINE of VIRTUE

Part II of The Metaphysic of Morals

With the Introduction to The Metaphysic of Morals
and the Preface to The Doctrine of Law

TRANSLATED WITH AN INTRODUCTION AND NOTES BY

MARY J. GREGOR

Foreword by H. J. Paton

UNIVERSITY OF PENNSYLVANIA PRESS

PHILADELPHIA

FOR MY PARENTS

CONTENTS

Foreword
by H. J. Paton

If we wish to understand Kant's moral philosophy as a whole, we must know something of the way in which he attempted to apply his fundamental moral principles to the particular virtues and duties of our everyday life. In his great ethical works—the *Groundwork of the Metaphysic of Morals* and the *Critique of Practical Reason*—this problem is reserved till later. There he is concerned only with the form of morality, with what he calls its supreme principle. If we may use a more simple idiom, he asks "What is moral goodness?"—not "What kinds of action are morally good?" Or again, he asks "What is Duty?"—not "What kinds of action are to be regarded as duties?"

It is true that in a few places he does refer to particular moral duties—negative duties, for example, like the duty not to commit suicide or the duty not to borrow money unless we intend to pay it back; and also positive duties like the duty to cultivate our talents or to show kindness to others. These are offered as illustrations of the way in which our ordinary moral judgments can be derived from his supreme moral principle; and without some such illustrations his whole discussion would be very much in the air. He may give some of us the impression that he thought the problem here to be much easier than it really is, but he makes it clear enough that his account of particular duties and their classification is only provisional.

In spite of these reservations the Anglo-Saxon mind, perhaps because of its practical bent, is apt to concentrate its attention on the application of Kant's moral principles rather than on the principles themselves. On the strength of a few hurried illustrations wholly fantastic structures have been built up. Some of these are merely trivial, like the widespread belief that Kant held suicide to be wrong on the ground that if everybody committed suicide, then there would be no one left to commit suicide. There is no trace of such a foolish argument in Kant himself, yet it has been extended, by what I can only call a stroke of genius, into something even more absurd. In one popular history of philosophy we have been solemnly assured that Kant thought it was wrong to borrow money because if we all tried to do so there would be no money left to borrow. Here the argument is as silly as the conclusion, and there is no trace of either in Kant. As I have said above, he thought it wrong to borrow money unless we intended to pay it back—a humdrum view with which most of us would presumably agree.

However trivial such misrepresentations may sound, they illustrate the tendency to invent imaginary ways of applying Kant's doctrine instead of studying the way in which he actually applied it himself. His own systematic applications of the supreme moral principle are to be found in his *Metaphysic of Morals* (which is not to be confused with his *Groundwork of the Metaphysic of Morals*). This is divided into two parts, the *Doctrine of Law* and the *Doctrine of Virtue;* and it is the second or purely ethical part that Mrs. Gregor has translated here (along with the introduction to the work as a whole). An attentive study of it should clear up many serious misunderstandings—for example, the common belief that for Kant goodness is wholly subordinate to duty, that the moral law is essentially an imperative, that the ends of action must be ignored, and that no place can be allowed to moral feeling.

The most serious misunderstanding of all is the view that Kant's argument is based on purely logical, as opposed to teleological, consistency: he is supposed to deduce all particular moral duties from the mere form of morality (or the mere form of law) without any regard to its matter, that is, to the ends of moral action. The flat contradiction of all this in the *Metaphysic of Morals* will come to many as a complete surprise. In the *Doctrine of Law* the problem is how to combine the arbitrary and often incompatible ends of individual men within a framework of law which aims at liberty. The *Doctrine of Virtue,* on the other hand, or ethics in the strict sense (as opposed to jurisprudence), is essentially concerned with ends which are also duties. Indeed ethics can even be defined as "the system of the ends of pure practical reason." If we ignore this doctrine in our interpretations of Kant's moral philosophy, we do so at our own peril; and it is the working out of this doctrine in detail which gives the *Metaphysic of Morals* its supreme interest.

It is astonishing that so important a part of Kant's moral system should have had to wait 160 years for an adequate translation into English; and perhaps it is not too cynical to suppose that its general neglect in English-speaking countries may have sprung partly from the difficulty of having to struggle with the German original. Mrs. Gregor has done a very great service in attempting to fill this gap, and it is to be hoped that such difficulties as may remain will be met by her forthcoming commentary.*

Kant himself thought that a *Metaphysic of Morals,* in

* M. J. Gregor: *Laws of Freedom,* Basil Blackwell (Oxford), 1963.

spite of its horrifying title, would be popular and even easy. His expectation, as it turns out, can hardly be said to have been fulfilled; but this is because in his Introductions he goes back again to his first principles, his definitions of terms, his principles of division and classification, and so on. His discussion of these throws precious light on his moral system, but without the aid of a commentary it is bound to be difficult for those who are not familiar with his doctrines, and perhaps even for those who are. When he settles down to examine particular virtues and duties, he becomes much more human; and the tyro in philosophy would be well advised to skip the long introductions and to concentrate on the main body of the book, leaving the more abstract discussions for study later. Some readers may prefer to see how a system works out concretely before they decide to face the effort necessary if they are to understand its professed basis and philosophical justification.

On the human side they may also like to get some idea of the author's own character and moral attitude, which is never wholly irrelevant to his philosophy; and this comes out most clearly in discussing particular problems. In this work they will find Kant, if I am not mistaken, to be a wise and kindly old man, limited no doubt by his own ideals and those of his age, as we are by ours, perhaps a little too austere and scholastic for modern taste, well aware of human weakness, yet very sensitive to the need for cherishing human dignity and self-respect both in oneself and in others. Special attention may be called to the "Casuistical Questions," in which he raises queries about possible exceptions to moral rules. He does not give us answers since the answers must be left to the judgment of the individual; but the questions themselves could hardly have been raised at all if Kant had been quite so rigorous as he is commonly supposed to be. Even as regards lying, where he can be seen at his most rigorous, he does not shun such questions, and the undercurrent of his dry humour almost comes to the surface when he considers how to deal with an author who asks us whether we like his work. Yet it must be admitted that his humour seems at times to be unconscious, as in some of the answers assigned to a child in his sketch of a moral catechism—perhaps they didn't sound quite so strange in the eighteenth century, but the early days when he had been a tutor to young children must have become rather remote. In spite of his extraordinary intellectual gifts he was by no means a demi-god, but rather a very human being whom it would be difficult not to like and perhaps even to love.

I hope Mrs. Gregor's translation will find the wide circle of readers that she and Kant deserve.

H. J. Paton

June 1961

Translator's Note

In this translation I have relied chiefly on the first edition of the *Metaphysic of Morals* (1797). The second edition (1803), published during Kant's lifetime but apparently without his co-operation, contains a number of emendations which, although often helpful, seem occasionally to distort Kant's meaning. These emendations are, for the most part, minor ones—*e.g.* the repetition of a noun—which coincide naturally with the translation. In the case of more extensive revisions which really clarify Kant's meaning, I have quoted the second edition in footnotes. Kant's notes, indicated by asterisks, are to be found within the text of the translation itself. My notes, indicated by numbers, are at the end of the translation. A bracketed number in the text indicates the end of the corresponding page in the edition of the Royal Prussian Academy in Berlin. All references in my *Introduction* are, again, to the volume and page of the Prussian Academy edition of Kant's works.

The two parts of the *Metaphysic of Morals*, the *Doctrine of Law* and the *Doctrine of Virtue*, were first published separately, the former containing an introduction to the whole of the *Metaphysic of Morals*, as well as a preface that is relevant to both parts of the work. The present translation contains this preface (to the *Doctrine of Law*), the *Introduction* to the *Metaphysic of Morals* as a whole, the *Preface to the Doctrine of Virtue*, the *Introduction to the*

Doctrine of Virtue, and the *Doctrine of Virtue* itself. Because it omits the *Doctrine of Law* and because the *Metaphysic of Morals* contains the difficulties peculiar to a hurriedly written and, in a sense, unfinished work, I have added a brief introduction designed to show the overall method of Kant's applied moral philosophy and to clarify certain points in the *Doctrine of Virtue*. Since this introduction is not intended as a complete commentary on the *Doctrine of Virtue*, it omits altogether or mentions only in passing many key points which are either self-explanatory or too complicated to be handled briefly. Yet some explanation, however fragmentary, may prove helpful to the reader when Kant sets his standards unreasonably high. A more detailed analysis of the *Metaphysic of Morals* can be found in my commentary on this work, *Laws of Freedom*.

I am most deeply indebted to Professor H. J. Paton for his generous advice, criticism, and encouragement throughout the time I was making this translation. I should also like to thank Professor Julius Ebbinghaus for his help in providing historical background material for some of my notes. The *Philosophische Bibliothek* edition of the *Metaphysic of Morals* has also proved helpful in this respect. Finally, I wish to acknowledge my indebtedness to the American Association of University Women who, by their award of the Margaret Snell Fellowship for the year 1959-1960, made this translation possible.

Mary J. Gregor

August 1963

Translator's Introduction

The Nature of a Metaphysic of Morals (pp. 211-228)

If a metaphysic of morals in general is an investigation of the *a priori* principles of pure practical reason or moral laws, then the *Groundwork of the Metaphysic of Morals* and the *Metaphysic of Morals* itself comprise the two parts of a metaphysic of morals. The purpose of the *Groundwork* is limited to investigating the supreme principle of morality, the ultimate criterion of right as well as of good for rational beings as such. The *Metaphysic of Morals* seeks to apply this principle systematically to human nature, in order to obtain from it a system of specifically human duties.

In Kant's view, the different purposes of the two works imply a corresponding difference in the types of knowledge contained in them. The supreme moral principle, he maintains, is "pure knowledge" or knowledge in which the concepts themselves, as well as the connection asserted between them, are derived independently of sense experience, merely from reason's reflection on its own activity. But in order to apply this principle to human nature, the *Metaphysic of Morals* must admit certain empirical concepts. Like all moral laws, these applied moral principles are *a priori* propositions: the connection asserted between the will and the moral necessity of certain maxims is not derived from experience. But, unlike the supreme moral principle, they are not pure knowledge because the concepts so connected are derived, in part, from sense experience.

There is, however, a limitation on the empirical elements admissible in a metaphysic of morals—a limitation which defines more precisely the scope of this work. Because Kant is aiming at an exhaustive classification of duties, he can admit into a metaphysic of morals only empirical knowledge of "men considered merely as men," knowledge of what belongs essentially to human nature as such. In this way he can, as in the earlier *Metaphysical First Principles of Natural Science*, give an *a priori* and so exhaustive classification of his subject matter. On the other hand, were he to admit knowledge of the contingent circumstances in which individual men may find themselves, duties would have to be classified on an empirical basis, where we can never hope to achieve systematic completeness. From this limitation it follows that a metaphysic of morals must remain on the level of duties binding upon all men as such, without considering formally the modifications which these moral laws may undergo in special circumstances. Kant envisages an appendix to the *Metaphysic of Morals* in which the moral laws for men as such would be "schematized," as it were, and made ready for their final application by judgment. But in the *Metaphysic of Morals* itself such problems can be handled only by way of "casuistical questions," with a view to the exercise and training of moral judgment.

While Kant's definition of "metaphysics" may be of a rather technical nature, his limitation on empirical elements in a metaphysic of morals has important consequences. First, it is relevant to the charge of rigorism often brought against him—the charge that he fails to provide for necessary exceptions to applied moral laws. We must remember that the prohibitions he formulates are intended to be

valid for "men considered merely as men," and that the
nature of the work prevents him from considering special
cases in which we might assert a moral title to perform a
generally prohibited action on the ground that failure to
perform the action would involve a violation of another
duty. Kant recognizes a distinction between arbitrary and
morally necessary exceptions to the laws of a metaphysic of
morals, but the scope of the work prevents him from considering the circumstances in which a "collision of grounds
of obligation" might occur. Secondly, Kant's procedure
indicates that his application of the supreme moral principle
is to be a systematic one, not a headlong plunge from the
ultimate criterion of morality to specific duties. The
Groundwork's silence regarding criteria for bringing actions under the supreme moral principle is perhaps the most
fruitful source of misunderstandings concerning Kant's
moral philosophy: it is undoubtedly the reason behind the
frequent assertions that the categorical imperative cannot
be applied. Yet the *Groundwork* states clearly that the
systematic derivation of particular duties is reserved for the
Metaphysic of Morals.

The *Groundwork*, as an analysis of the formal element
present in every morally good action, arrived at the conclusion that while right action is action upon a maxim which
could serve as universal law, morally good action is right
action in which the thought of the universal validity of the
maxim serves as the motive determining our choice. In the
Metaphysic of Morals Kant wishes to derive from this
supreme moral principle two systems of duties: Law, the
system of those duties which can be enforced by legal
sanctions and so can be fulfilled independently of our
moral attitude of will; and ethics, the system of those duties
which our pure practical reason alone can constrain us to

fulfill from the motive of duty. Hence he must first prescind from any reference to the agent's motive and regard the categorical imperative simply as the law of rational will as such, without specifying whether it is the agent's own will or the will of another. This abstraction gives us "universal practical philosophy," a study of the basic moral concepts prior to their qualification as juridical or ethical, which stands between the *Groundwork* and the Doctrines of Law and Virtue. Having thus obtained the first principle of all duty, the formal principle of action "so act that your maxim could become a universal law," he can consider it first as the principle of laws that arise in outer or juridical legislation, then as the principle of duties that arise in inner or ethical legislation.

The fact that the supreme moral principle is the law of freedom, which merely expresses the condition of free or rational action as such, determines the character of Kant's applied moral philosophy. Because all moral laws must be derived from this principle, both juridical and ethical laws must be "laws of freedom," laws which prescribe the conditions under which freedom can be realized in one or another aspect of our actions. Since juridical legislation can attach to the law only constraint through motives of sensuous origin, and since the moral goodness of an action is located in its pure rational motive, laws that arise in juridical legislation must be conditions of the freedom which can be achieved independently of the subject's moral attitude of will. They are laws of "outer freedom," the conditions under which each subject of the law can realize the relative freedom manifested in action toward whatever ends he may have set for himself. Ethical laws, on the other hand, will be those that arise directly in inner legislation, in which pure practical reason provides not only the law but also the constraint accompanying the law. Since this legislation is concerned with the moral goodness of our will, ethical laws will be conditions of "inner freedom," a state in which choice is free from the influence of the inclinations as such and open to that of pure practical reason with its motive of duty.

If, as the *Doctrine of Law* establishes, juridical laws are principles of pure practical reason, it is clear that they are always accompanied by ethical obligation, the constraint of pure practical reason to act from the motive of duty. So far as Law is concerned, we fulfill our duty if we act on a material maxim that could become a universal law of outer freedom. But ethics adds the requirement that we make the thought of the universal validity of the maxim our formal maxim in acting. Ethics on its formal side is thus concerned with all our duties, whether they arise directly in ethical legislation or whether, originating in juridical legislation as conditions of outer freedom, they are adopted into ethical legislation in so far as the thought that they are duties is prescribed as our motive in fulfilling them.

The Content of the Doctrine of Virtue (*pp. 379-388*)

But on its material side, as a system of duties, ethics is the doctrine of those duties which arise directly in ethical legislation as conditions of inner freedom. Such duties, Kant argues, consist in obligatory ends, ends which it is a duty for us to have. For, since it is the ends which we adopt on the basis of our sensuous inclinations that lead us to violate the moral law, pure practical reason can check the influence of the inclinations on choice only by subordinating our subjective ends to its own system of pure rational ends. Such obligatory ends are properly called "duties of virtue" and this, apparently, for two reasons: first, that they are conditions of inner freedom on which virtue is based, and secondly, that only a virtuous attitude of will can lead us to fulfill these duties, since it is both logically and morally impossible for us to be compelled by others to adopt certain ends. On its formal side, ethics is the doctrine of virtue, *i.e.* of the strength of our moral attitude of will. On its material side, it is the doctrine of duties of virtue; for in relation to the various objects of a moral will and the inclinations that must be overcome in pursuing these objects, our one virtuous attitude of will is differentiated into a number of particular virtues.

The crucial argument of the *Doctrine of Virtue* is that from the formal principle of all duty, so act that your maxim could become universal law, to the special first principle of ethical duty, act according to a maxim of ends which you could will everyone to have. The first principle of all duty abstracts altogether from ends; but by considering the nature of human action as such, we can derive from this principle, regarded in ethics as the law of our own will, a categorical imperative regarding our ends.

From Kant's definition of an end as "an object of free choice, the thought of which determines choice to an action by which the object is produced," it follows that human action is essentially purposive: there can be no human action without an end. Now when Kant points out that the setting of any end is "an act of freedom, not an operation of nature," he is integrating the present argument with the *Groundwork*'s discussion of objective principles of practical reason. According to the *Groundwork*, free or human action is action on a maxim or subjective principle of practical reason, which comes under objective principles expressing the way in which a fully rational being would act and the way in which an imperfectly rational being ought to

xxii

act. If adopting a maxim is equivalent to setting an end, then our adoption of ends comes under objective principles of practical reason, and it remains for Kant to show that if we are subject to an unconditioned principle of action we are subject at the same time to a categorical imperative regarding our ends.

Conditioned objective principles of practical reason regard the end as given on the basis of inclination and prescribe as rationally necessary such actions as are the appropriate means to that end. According to them, no action is rationally necessary in itself: its necessity is contingent upon our having the end to which the action is the means. Now, since there is no action without an end, if we could adopt ends only on the basis of our inclinations our maxims would be subject only to conditioned imperatives, and a categorical imperative regarding our actions would be impossible. But it is a "fact of reason" that certain actions are unconditionally necessary according to principles of pure practical reason, without reference to the ends of inclination. Hence there must also be ends of pure practical reason and, corresponding to them, a categorical imperative commanding us to adopt our ends on the basis of their universal validity. In short, the relation of ends to actions is such that, if there are actions that are necessary according to pure rational principles, there must also be ends that are necessary according to principles of pure practical reason.

The will determined to action by the thought of its universal validity must, then, adopt ends on the basis of their universal validity; and the question now arises: what are the ends of pure practical reason? From the second *Critique* we know that, given the nature of reason as a systematizing power, the complete object of pure practical reason is the *summum bonum*, which consists in the perfection and happiness of finite rational beings. The first principle of ethics is, in fact, a command to promote the *summum bonum*. But if we ask what elements in the highest good it is our duty to promote, we find that obligatory ends are limited to our own perfection and the happiness of other men.

As beings capable of rational and moral action, we rationally will to develop our capacities, first for setting and realizing ends in general (our natural perfection) and secondly for setting ends or determining ourselves to action independently of inclination as such (our moral perfection). But since "I ought" implies "I can," and since each man's perfection is the work of his own freedom, it cannot be our duty to promote the perfection of other men. Again, as beings with needs and wants we rationally will their total satisfaction, *i.e.* happiness. But since an obligatory end implies constraint to a reluctantly adopted end, and since every man necessarily and spontaneously wills his own happiness, our duty in this regard is limited to promoting the happiness of other men. To pursue one's own happiness, subject to the limiting condition of morality, is permissible and can be morally good; but it is not a duty.

Kant subsequently argues that we have a duty of refraining from scandal—that is, from tempting others to vice; but this he subsumes under the obligatory end of other men's happiness, which includes their freedom from the pangs of conscience. Again, he admits that we can have an indirect duty of promoting our own happiness, which is, however, a direct duty of promoting our moral perfection. If we have inclinations to, *e.g.*, intemperance, avarice, and laziness, it is our duty to take as our ends health, enjoyment of the goods of life, and prosperity, which are elements in human happiness from an objective point of view (though we refuse to regard them as elements in our happiness). But the ground for this duty is that sickness, misery, and poverty are temptations to vice, and if we have a duty to pursue their opposites, it is in order to preserve our moral integrity. By these qualifications Kant succeeds in maintaining that our obligatory ends are limited to our own natural and moral perfection and the happiness of other men.

Characteristics of Ethical Laws (pp. 388-396)

Unlike juridical laws, which prescribe definite actions as duties, ethical laws prescribe only that we adopt maxims of promoting our obligatory ends. Postponing his exposition of "wide" or "imperfect" duties, Kant discusses this principle in terms of the distinctive addition which ethics makes to the system of moral laws. Apart from obligatory ends and the ethical laws enjoining them, moral laws would all be essentially negative and limiting principles. It is obligatory ends that introduce into ethics positive and widening principles of duty.

The formal principle of action, "so act that your maxim of action could become a universal law," abstracts altogether from ends. Nor, Kant repeats, is the situation changed when, within ethics, we regard this principle as the law of our own will, that is, as accompanied by ethical obligation: it still prescribes no end in the positive sense of some state of affairs to be brought into being by our action. And since there is no maxim without an end, it prescribes no maxims of action but requires only that we reject such of our maxims of self-love as cannot qualify for giving universal law. Since our actions are means to ends, so long as duty is concerned only with actions in abstraction from ends we must regard our ends, and hence our maxims, as given on the basis of self-love. Duty, accordingly, consists only in limiting our pursuit of happiness to the condition that our maxims are consistent with universal law.

It is only by the concept of an obligatory end that we move from this limiting condition on our actions to laws commanding us to adopt certain maxims. It should be noted that when Kant distinguishes between "maxims of actions" and "maxims of ends" he is not speaking of two different kinds of maxims. A maxim of action is a principle of realizing an end through an action. But the fact that the first principle of all duty abstracts from ends, and only the principle of duties which arise in ethical legislation can deal with ends, means that for purposes of analysis he must distinguish between that aspect of our maxim which is subject to the formal principle of action and that which comes under the principle of ends. In any maxim of action toward an end—whether the end is an end of inclination or an obligatory end—the action is subject only to the limiting principle of action. It is the first principle of ethical duty that brings ends under moral laws and, in so doing, commands us to adopt certain maxims. Laws derived from the formal principle of action prescribe no ends, and neither do ethical laws prescribe determinate actions. On the latter part of this assertion Kant bases his notion of wide duty.

If juridical laws are derived merely from the formal condition of lawfulness as such, they must determine precise actions as duties. Juridical duties are just the actions necessary in order to avoid coming into conflict with universal law; and since it is never permissible to act in such a way that our maxim could not become universal law, juridical laws cannot permit arbitrary exceptions to the law nor can they leave it to the subject's free choice to determine the

xxvi

way in which and the extent to which he will act in ful-fillment of the law. Juridical duties are, in short, perfect duties of strict obligation.

From the fact that ethical laws go beyond the formal principle of action it follows that they prescribe wide or imperfect duties. If the law commands, not a specific action, but only the adoption of a purpose, it leaves a "latitude" or "play-room" for free choice in determining the action by which we shall realize the purpose—a latitude for deciding whether we shall, here and now, act toward this end and, if so, what and how much we shall do toward the end. We do not violate the law commanding us to make the happiness of others our end if we decide, here and now, not to comply with another's wishes or to do less than we might do. Since ethical laws prescribe maxims and not precise actions, transgressions of ethical laws consist not in omitting actions but rather in adopting maxims of indifference to obligatory ends. We transgress an ethical law either by lack of resoluteness in pursuing our moral purposes (in which case the transgression is moral weakness) or by re-fusing to adopt the obligatory end (in which case the transgression is vice).

But on what grounds are we entitled, in given circum-stances, to omit action in pursuit of an obligatory end or to do less than we could do? Can our refusal be an arbitrary one, based on inclination? Or is it only the existence of a conflicting ground of obligation that gives us the moral title to refuse to do the maximum possible, in any given situation, toward realizing the obligatory end? The *Groundwork* suggested that the latitude of imperfect duties implies permission to make arbitrary exceptions. The *Meta-physic of Morals* could be interpreted in the opposite way, since Kant here notes that a wide duty does not imply "a permission for exceptions to the maxims of actions, but only a permission to limit one maxim of duty by another (*e.g.* love of one's neighbor in general by love of one's parents) . . ."

But it is not necessary to interpret the text in this rigoristic way. Kant has distinguished carefully between an ethical law "which prescribes maxims of actions" (*e.g.* I will promote the happiness of others) and a juridical law "which prescribes actions themselves" (*e.g.* the repayment of debts). Hence his assertion that ethical laws do not allow us to make "exceptions to the maxims of actions" seems to mean merely that we are not allowed to give up the end altogether, not even on the ground that a contrary obligation excuses us from the pursuit of that end. We cannot assert that our obligation to help our parents is so great as to excuse us completely from the purpose of promoting the happiness of people other than our parents. Although Kant is not perfectly clear on this point, the contrary, rigoristic view of imperfect duty seems to blur the distinction between perfect and imperfect duty, to circumscribe sharply the element of spontaneity in moral action which Kant stresses, and to leave the way open to the attitude which he condemns as "fantastic virtue."

Perfect Duties to Oneself (pp. 419-421)

Ethics as a system of duties, Kant has said, is the doctrine of duties of virtue; and from the preceding paragraphs it follows that duties of virtue are imperfect duties. Yet a considerable part of the *Doctrine of Virtue* is taken up with "perfect duties to oneself," and some attempt must be made to account for the presence of these within Kant's ethics. If there are ethical prohibitions against certain uses of one's own person, such as suicide and intemperance, it is clear that these laws, in so far as they prescribe duties to oneself, cannot belong to the *Doctrine of Law*, which is concerned only with duties of outer freedom. Yet these perfect duties to oneself—which Kant sometimes calls "inner juridical duties" following from "the right of humanity in one's own person"—seem too closely analogous to juridical duties to belong in a positive way to the *Doctrine of Virtue*.

A partial solution to the difficulty is to be found in the *Nachlass* relevant to the *Metaphysic of Morals*. There Kant explains that perfect duties to oneself can be considered from two points of view, "according to their content" and "in themselves" (XXIII, 385). To view them according to their content is to abstract from the legislation in which they arise and consider only the principle from which they are derived. Since this principle is neither the first principle of Law nor the first principle of ethics but rather the first principle of all duty as such, perfect duties to oneself, according to their content, belong neither to the *Doctrine of Law* nor to the *Doctrine of Virtue* but rather to "moral philosophy in general," the study of personality as the highest limiting condition. Considered in themselves, however, they arise in ethical legislation, as conditions of inner freedom, and so belong to the *Doctrine of Virtue*.

Moreover Kant indicates, in the *Doctrine of Virtue*, that perfect duties to oneself are "duties of virtue" in a wider sense of the term. The distinguishing mark of a duty of virtue is that it involves the pursuit of an end, and the *Nachlass* again indicates that the relationship between perfect duties to oneself and ends is what entitles these duties to be called duties of virtue in a wide sense (XXIII, 383, 388, 398). An end is the "objective determining ground of choice," as a motive is its subjective determining ground.

Because perfect duties to oneself arise in the legislation that connects the motive of duty with the law, we cannot fulfill these duties without taking as our end the ground of obligation for these duties, namely the preservation of the integrity of our own person, which is the object of our choice. This is the negative and formal aspect of "the end of humanity in our own person," as the promotion of natural and moral perfection is its positive aspect; and it is this connection that enables Kant to call ethical duties of omission duties of virtue in a wider sense.

Since the main problem in Kant's discussions of perfect duties to oneself is that of the criteria by which he applies the supreme moral principle, I shall limit this part of the analysis to a statement of what I think these subordinate principles to be, using the specific vices prohibited only as illustrations of them. Kant divides perfect duties to oneself into two classes: duties to oneself as a moral being with an animal nature and duties to oneself merely as a moral being.

Perfect Duties to Oneself as a Moral Being
with an Animal Nature
(*Self-Murder, Self-Abuse, Intemperance: pp. 421-428*)

The form of the categorical imperative operative here is that which prohibits the use of persons, and more specifically of our own person, as a mere means to our subjective ends. This formula forbids, in terms of the *Doctrine of Virtue*, such actions as would be an "abasement of our personality." Whether this is strictly equivalent to the supreme moral principle or whether (as I believe) it is already an application of it need not concern us here. As the *Groundwork* shows, the formula of humanity as an end in itself can be derived from the formula of universal law.

xxx

But how are we to determine what actions are abasements of our personality? Kant offers three principles.

The first is implicit in his definition of all these vices as total or partial suicide. In each of these vices, Kant thinks, we are arbitrarily destroying or impairing our capacity for rational action (for setting and realizing ends in general), and hence indirectly our capacity for moral action. This is clear in the case of total self-murder (suicide for the sake of mere inclination), together with questions of self-mutilation for profit. As for self-abuse, Kant argues (in *Pädagogik*, p. 497) that the practice of this vice results in sterility, early old age, *etc.* Intemperance (drunkenness and gluttony) is a temporary hindering of the use of either reason itself or of our powers for skilful and reflective action in pursuit of our ends. And it is irrational arbitrarily to destroy or impair our capacities for rational action; in other words, the maxims of these vices cannot qualify for a giving of universal law.

The second principle is implicit in the division of these duties on the basis of the animal instincts for self-preservation, sex, and nourishment. In the realm of nature (as opposed to freedom) the instincts lead the animal to perform such actions as will result in the preservation of the animal itself, of the species, and of the animal's strength and powers. The presence of practical reason in man enables him to divert the instincts from their natural functions or to use them for the sake of mere pleasure in such a way as to destroy the subject, prevent the propagation of the species, or weaken the subject's powers. If the results toward which man's animal instincts naturally tend—the preservation of the animal substratum of moral action—are at the same time objective, rational ends of a moral being with an animal nature, then it is irrational to use the instincts unnaturally or in such a way as to frustrate these ends merely for the sake of pleasure.

Closely related to the second principle is the teleological view of nature implicit in Kant's discussions of duties. The human mind, he holds, is so constituted that we cannot explain organisms except by conceiving of them as natural purposes, *i.e.* as effects of an intelligent cause which produces them in accordance with ideas. This is not to assert that organisms are, in fact, effects of an intelligent cause: it is only by analogy that we conceive of them in this way. But we must think of the organism, with its instincts and powers, as ordered by nature to some end; and in the case of the instincts nature's purposes are, again, the preservation of the individual, of the species, and of the individual's powers. Hence it is immoral to use an instinct contrary to "nature's purpose."

The crucial question regarding Kant's method is that of the relationship among these principles. It would seem that the first principle alone—the definition of these actions as total or partial suicide—is sufficient to establish the irrationality and hence the immorality of the actions; and Kant does appear, in the case of each vice, to regard this as the "rational proof." His further points—that the actions involve the use of the instincts contrary to nature and nature's purposes—are not independent proofs but rather convenient means for "gaining entrance" for the rational proof into the "common understanding." Given the character of popular ethics in Kant's time and the 18th century's acceptance of a teleological nature, Kant could expect to win a more favorable hearing for his ethics by connecting it with "nature" and the Stoic dictum "live according to nature." It would appear that, at least according to Kant's original plan, nature and its purposes have no moral signifi-

xxxii

cance of their own and play no part in the moral proof itself. Their relevance lies only in the fact that they coincide with the objective ends of an animal-moral being and so can be used as a device for popularizing applied moral philosophy. At the same time it must be admitted that Kant occasionally tends, in his discussion of specific duties, to stress the teleological aspects of the exposition at the expense of the rational proof itself.

Perfect Duties to Oneself Merely as a Moral Being (Lying, Avarice, False Humility, pp. 429-442)

The vices of this category consist not so much in particular actions as rather in basic principles which are directly opposed to the prerogative of a moral being, inner freedom. By the "inner lie" we deceive ourselves regarding the unconditioned nature of the moral law and hence about the moral worth of our actions; in servile avarice we subject our attitude of mind to our desire for riches and make an end of something that, in itself, has the value only of a means to the rational end of happiness; in false humility we waive our claim to the respect to which we are entitled as moral beings, in order to gain favor with other men. All such principles imply, in a practical sense, a false valuation of ourselves and of our inner worth as subjects of pure practical reason, and hence fail to qualify for a giving of universal law.

As juridical duties provide the basic framework of non-interference with one another's ends, within which we can fulfill our ethical duties of actively helping others to achieve their ends, so perfect duties to ourselves prohibit the destruction of our animal and moral being and are thus the condition under which we can fulfill our imperfect duties to ourselves of striving for natural and moral perfection.

Although these latter duties involve difficulties, they are of a somewhat technical nature, and the problem of our duties of virtue to others claims more attention.

Duties of Virtue to Others (*pp. 448-450 and 462 ff.*)

In the case of duties of virtue to others we face a problem which is similar, in some respects, to the difficulty concerning perfect duties to oneself. For these duties to others include not only our pursuit of their happiness (duties of love) but also duties of respect. Like perfect duties to oneself, these duties of respect are analogous to juridical duties in so far as they consist in refraining from anything (*e.g.* manifestations of contempt, backbiting, ridicule) which would detract from the respect to which others, as men, are entitled. Yet Kant seems to say that duties of respect are really imperfect duties: it is only in relation to duties of love that they are considered strict or narrow.

In order to explain, first, the distinction of duties of respect from juridical duties and, secondly, their character as imperfect duties, we should note that in the case of duties of respect the law does not so much prohibit actions as rather enjoin an attitude toward other men. The law prescribes, immediately, a maxim of limiting our demands on others through our recognition of their dignity as moral agents, and only through the medium of this maxim does it prohibit certain actions. If we refrain from showing contempt for others only out of prudence, while still despising them inwardly, we are really violating our duties of respect. And it is for this reason that duties of respect, unlike juridical duties, cannot be enforced by external compulsion.

However, while this point clearly distinguishes duties of respect from juridical duties, it does not yet account for their character as duties of virtue, since the maxim of respect still does not seem to be one of realizing some end. In order to resolve this difficulty, we must consider Kant's view that in fulfilling our duties of virtue to others we are striving to realize an "intelligible" or moral world, in which love and respect are analogous to the forces of attraction and repulsion in the physical world. The maxims of love and respect are abstractions from the maxim of realizing correct moral relations among men; and while they can, for purposes of analysis, be considered separately, practical love and respect cannot exist separately as moral relations. They are always united in any duty of virtue to others, although now the one and now the other will predominate, thus giving one duty the title "duty of love" and another "duty of respect." To perform a service of love for another without taking care to leave him his independence would not really be to fulfill a duty of love to him; and again, in fulfilling a duty of respect we must not merely refrain from anything that would deprive another of the respect due him, but must do so out of concern for his moral well-being (which, Kant has argued, is an element in his happiness). It is only by abstraction that we can speak of maxims of love and respect; the maxim from which both are derived is that of "friendship," a mixture of practical love and respect which describes men's relations in the moral world. And the realization of this world is an obligatory end.

The *Metaphysic of Morals*, then, deals with the four main types of duty: juridical duty, perfect duty to oneself, imperfect duty to oneself, and duty of virtue to others. These duties, the matter of moral laws, are the conditions of outer and inner freedom respectively. To them the *Doctrine of Virtue* adds ethical obligation or constraint through the thought of duty and so directs the will to the realization of the highest good, the system of the ends of pure practical reason. These, then, are the pivotal concepts of the *Metaphysic of Morals;* and with Kant's exposition of them we are finally in a position to judge the applicability of his supreme moral principle.

MARY J. GREGOR

THE DOCTRINE OF VIRTUE

Part II of

The Metaphysic of Morals

With the Introduction to The Metaphysic of Morals
and the Preface to The Doctrine of Law

PREFACE
to the
Doctrine of Law

As [the *Critique of Pure Reason*] was followed by the metaphysical first principles of *natural science*, so the *Critique of Practical Reason* should be followed by the metaphysical first principles of the *doctrine of Law* and the metaphysical first principles of the *doctrine of virtue*, which together make up the system of the metaphysic of morals. The following Introduction to the *Metaphysic of Morals* presents and, to some extent, illustrates the form which the system will take in both these parts.

The doctrine of Law, the first part of moral philosophy, requires a system proceeding from reason, which could be called a *metaphysic of Law*. But because the pure concept of Law still looks to practice (application to cases that come up in experience), the divisions of a *metaphysical* system of Law would also have to take into account the empirical manifold of these cases. Only in this way can it make the division complete, as is essential in constructing a system of reason. But the empirical does not admit of an exhaustive division, and if we aim at this completeness (intending at least to approximate to it), we cannot bring empirical concepts into the system as integral parts of it, but only as examples in the notes. So the appropriate title for the first part of the *Metaphysic of Morals* will be only the *Metaphysical First Principles of the Doctrine of Law;* for in applying those principles to empirical cases we cannot expect to achieve the system itself: the most we can expect is to approximate to it. Accordingly we shall handle this as we did the (earlier) metaphysical first principles of natural science: the Law that belongs to the system traced out *a priori* will go into the text, while the laws drawn from particular cases of experience will be put into notes, [205] which will sometimes be extensive. Otherwise it would be hard to distinguish what is metaphysics from what belongs to empirical practice of Law.

We hear often enough the charge that writers of philosophical treaties make them obscure and even deliberately unintelligible, as a masquerade for deep insight. I can best anticipate and forestall this charge by gladly complying with the duty which Herr Garve, a philosopher in the true sense of the word, lays upon the philosophical writer. My only reservation is imposed by the nature of science itself, which is to correct and increase our knowledge.

This wise man rightly insists (in his work entitled *Vermischte Aufsätze,* page 352 ff.) that a philosophical writer is open to the suspicion of being muddled in his own concepts unless he can make his work *popular* (that is, sufficiently concrete to be communicated to everybody). I freely admit this requirement, and except from it only the systematic critique of the power of reason itself, along with what can be established only through the conclusions of a critique; for this concerns the distinction of the sensible in our knowledge from reason's [Ideas of the] supersensible. This can never be put into popular form—no formal metaphysics can—although its results can be made quite clear to the sound reason (of an unwitting metaphysician).

Popularity (popular language) is out of the question here; on the contrary, we must insist on scholastic *precision*, even if we are charged with hair-splitting (for using the *language of the schools*). For only by such precision can precipitate reason be brought to understand itself and give up its dogmatic assertions.

But if *pedants* presume to address the public (from pulpits or in popular writings) in technical terms which belong only in the schools, the Critical philosopher is no more responsible for their behaviour than is the grammarian for the folly of quibblers (*logodaedalus*). Here ridicule can hit only the man, not the science.

To say that before the advent of Critical Philosophy there was as yet no philosophy at all sounds arrogant, egoistic, and disparaging to those who still cling to their old systems. [206]—To clear ourselves of this supposed effrontery, we must ask *whether there could really be more than one philosophy*. There have been different ways of philosophizing and of going back to the first principles of reason in order to base a system, more or less successfully, on them; indeed there must be many experiments of this kind, each of which has its merit in its own time. But since, to consider the matter objectively, there can be only *one* human reason, there cannot be many philosophies: in other words, there can be only *one* true system of philosophy from principles, no matter in how many different and even contradictory ways men may have philosophized about one and the same proposition. So the *moralist* is justified in saying that there is only *one* doctrine of virtue—that is, one single system that connects all duties of virtue by a principle; the *chemist*, that there is only *one* chemistry (*Lavoisier's*); the *teacher of medicine*, that there is only *one* principle for systematically classifying diseases (*Brown's*).

Although the new system excludes all others, its advocates do not, in asserting this, detract from the merit of the older moralists, chemists, and teachers of medicine; for without their discoveries and even their miscarried attempts we should not have succeeded in unifying the whole of philosophy in one system according to its true principle.—Thus anyone who originates a system of philosophy says, in effect, that before his philosophy there was no philosophy at all. For were he willing to admit that there had been another (and a true) one, then there would be two different and true philosophies on one and the same subject; and this is self-contradictory.—Accordingly when the Critical Philosophy proclaims itself a philosophy such that before it there was as yet no philosophy at all, it does nothing more than what every new philosophy has done, will do, and in fact must do.

The charge that a doctrine which essentially distinguishes the Critical Philosophy is not original to it and may have been borrowed from another philosophy (or mathematics) would be *less* important but not altogether negligible. A reviewer from Tübingen claims to have discovered something of this sort in a doctrine of the Critical Philosophy which concerns the definition of philosophy as such: namely, that what the author of the *Critique of Pure Reason* gives out as his own—and not inconsiderable—discovery was put forward many years ago by someone else, in almost the same words.* [207] I leave it to anyone to

---

* *Porro de actuali constructione hic non quaeritur, cum ne possint quidem sensibiles figurae ad rigorem definitionem effingi; sed requiritur cognitio eorum, quibus absolvitur formatio, quae intellectualis quaedam constructio est.* C. A. Hausen, *Elem. Mathes.*, Pars I, p. 86 A 1734. [Moreover, we are not speaking here of the actual construction, since perceptible figures cannot be devised according to the strictness of definitions; we are rather seeking knowledge of what goes to make up the figure, and this is, as it were, a construction made by the understanding.]

4

judge whether the words *intellectualis quaedam constructio* could have yielded the notion of *exhibiting a given concept in a priori intuition*—a notion which at one stroke clearly distinguishes philosophy from mathematics. I am sure that Hausen himself would not have allowed his term to be interpreted in this way. The possibility of an *a priori* intuition implies that space is an *a priori* intuition and not, as Wolff explains it, a mere juxtaposition of the manifold outside one another, given in empirical intuition; and Hausen, not wanting to get involved in far-reaching philosophical investigations, would have been frightened away by it. To this acute mathematician the "construction," as it were, made by the understanding means nothing more than the (empirical) *drawing* of a *line* [inadequately] corresponding to a concept, an unavoidable deviation from which the mathematician abstracts in the proof itself, attending only to the rule. This can be perceived, again, in the "construction" of equations in geometry.

So far as the spirit of Critical Philosophy is concerned, the *least* important consideration is the mischief that certain of its imitators have made by using its terms—which in the *Critique of Pure Reason* itself cannot be replaced by more customary words—outside the *Critique*, for the free exchange of thought. This, in any case, deserves to be blamed, as Herr Nicolai censures it, although he will reserve his own judgment as to whether these terms should be used in their own proper field, where they may merely conceal a general poverty of thought.[1]—However, the *unpopular pedant* does deserve to be laughed at more than the *un-Critical ignoramus* (and the metaphysician who clings obstinately to his old system, heedless of all critique, can really be considered ignorant, even though he simply *ignores* arbitrarily what he wants to prevent from spreading because it does not belong to his older school of thought).

5

But if it is true, as [208] Shaftesbury holds, that a doctrine's ability to withstand *ridicule* may well be a touch-stone of its truth (especially in the case of a practical doctrine), then the Critical Philosophy's turn must finally come. And it will have the *last* and so the *best* laugh when it sees one after another of the long-established systems collapsing like a house of cards and its hangers-on scattering—a fate they cannot avoid.

Toward the end of the book I have worked up certain chapters with less fulness of detail than would be expected on the basis of the earlier ones—partly because it seemed to me that they can be easily inferred from the earlier ones and partly, too, because the later chapters (dealing with Public Law) are still subject to so much debate, and yet so important, that they can well postpone final judgment for a time.

I hope that I shall soon be able to provide the meta-physical first principles of the doctrine of virtue.[2]

INTRODUCTION
to the
Metaphysic of Morals

ON THE RELATION OF THE POWERS OF THE
HUMAN MIND TO MORAL LAWS

The *appetitive power* is the power to cause the objects of one's mental representations by means of these same representations. The power of a being to act in accordance with its representations is called *life*.

To begin with, an act of appetite or aversion is always connected with *pleasure* or *pain*, the capacity for which is called *feeling*. But the converse is not always true. For there can be a pleasure which is not connected with any appetite for the object, but simply with the mere representation which we form of an object (without regard to whether the object exists or not). And, secondly, pleasure or pain at the object of the appetite does not always precede the act of the appetite and need not always be its cause. The pleasure or pain can also be the effect of the appetitive act.

But we call the capacity for pleasure or pain at a representation "*feeling*" because both of these comprise what is *merely subjective* in the relation to our representation and contain no reference to an object which could give us knowledge of the object* (or even knowledge of our own [211] state). Even sensations have, over and above the quality (of e.g. red or sweet) added to them by the subject's nature, a reference to an object, which is part of our knowledge of the object. But pleasure or pain (at red or sweet) expresses nothing at all in the object, but simply a relation to the subject. For this reason we cannot give a more precise description of pleasure and pain in themselves. We can at most only make them recognizable in usage by citing the results they have in certain relations.

Pleasure is *practical* if it is necessarily connected with appetite (for an object whose representation affects feeling in this way); the pleasure may be either the cause or the effect of the appetitive act. But if the pleasure is not connected with appetite for an object and so is not basically a pleasure in the existence of the object represented, but one that is attached to the representation taken simply by itself, it can be called a merely contemplative pleasure or *inactive satisfaction*. The feeling of contemplative pleasure is called *taste*. If practical philosophy speaks of contemplative pleasure at all, it mentions it only in passing, and not as if the concept were indigenous to it. As for practical pleasure, the

---

* Sensibility in general is the subjective aspect of our representations; for it is understanding that first refers the representations to an object or *thinks* something through them. Now sensibility has two sides: sense and feeling. If the subjective element in our representations can be referred to an object for knowledge of it (either knowledge of its form, in which case it is pure intuition, or knowledge of its matter, in which case it is sensation), then sensibility, as receptivity to this representation, is *sense*. But if the subjective aspect of our representation cannot become *part of our knowledge* because it is merely the reference of the representation to the *subject* and contains nothing that can be utilized for knowledge of the object, then this receptivity to the representation is called *feeling*. Feeling is the effect of the representation (which may be either sensuous or intellectual) on the subject, and it belongs to sensibility, although the representation itself may belong to understanding or reason.

act of the appetitive power which is preceded and caused by the pleasure is called *desire* in the narrow sense, while habitual desire is called *inclination*. If understanding judges the connection of the pleasure with the appetitive power to be valid according to a general rule (but valid only for the subject), this connection is called an *interest*. In the case of desire, the practical pleasure must accordingly be called an interest of the inclination. But if the pleasure can only follow from a preceding act of the appetitive power, then it is an intellectual pleasure and the interest in the object is an interest of reason. For if the interest were sensuous and not based merely on pure rational principles, [212] then the pleasure would have to have sensation connected with it in order to determine the appetitive power. In cases where we must admit a pure rational interest, we cannot substitute any interest of inclination for it; but to conform with the common use of language, we can speak of inclination to what can be an object only of intellectual pleasure— a habitual appetite proceeding from a pure rational interest. But a *non-sensuous inclination* of this sort (*propensio intellectualis*) would not be the cause of this pure rational interest, but rather its effect.

Furthermore, we must distinguish *concupiscence* (sensuality), as that which stimulates the appetitive act, from the appetite itself. It is always a sensuous function of the mind, but it is not itself able to produce any act of the appetitive power.

The appetitive power which acts in accordance with concepts, in so far as the ground determining it to action lies in itself and not in the object, is called a power *to act or to refrain from acting at one's discretion*. It is called *choice* [*Willkür*] when it is joined with consciousness that its action can produce the object; otherwise its act is called a *wish.* The appetitive power whose inner determining ground, and so the decision itself, lies in the subject's reason is called the *will* [*Wille*]. The will is therefore the appetitive power viewed in relation to the ground that determines the power of choice to the action, while the power of choice is the appetitive power viewed in relation to the action. The will itself has, properly speaking, no determining ground: in so far as reason can determine the power of choice, the will is, rather, practical reason itself.

In as much as reason can determine the appetitive power as such, the will can include under itself not only *choice* but also mere *wish.* The power of choice that can be determined by *pure reason* is called free choice [*freie Willkür*]. That which can be determined only by *inclination* (sensuous impulse, *stimulus*) would be animal choice (*arbitrium brutum*). Human choice is such that, while it can be *affected* by impulses, it cannot be *determined* by them. Hence in itself (apart from an acquired facility of reason) it is not pure, but it can still be determined to actions by pure will. *Freedom* of choice is this independence from sensuous impulse in the determination of choice. This is the negative concept of freedom. The positive concept of freedom is that of the [213] power of pure reason to be of itself practical. But pure reason can be practical only if the maxim of every action is subjected to the condition that it qualifies as a universal law. For as pure reason applied to the power of choice without regard to the object of choice, in as much as it is a power of principles (here of practical principles—hence in as much as it is a legislative power) it can make only the form of the maxim, its fitness for universal law, into the first principle and determining ground of choice, since the matter of the law is excluded. And since the maxims of men, based on subjective grounds, do not of themselves agree with that objective ground, pure practical reason can lay down this law only as an imperative that commands or prohibits absolutely.

These laws of freedom (as distinguished from laws of nature) are called *moral*. In so far as they have to do only with mere external actions and their lawfulness they are called *juridical* laws; but if they also require that they themselves (the laws) be the ground determining choice to actions, then they are *ethical* laws. So we say that conformity with juridical law comprises the *legality* of the action, and conformity with ethical law, its *morality*. In so far as choice is determined by laws of reason, its exercise is free. But the freedom to which juridical laws refer can be only freedom in the outer exercise of choice, whereas the freedom with which ethical laws are concerned is freedom in both the outer and the inner exercise of choice. In theoretical philosophy it is said that only objects of outer sense are in space, whereas all objects—those of outer as well as of inner sense—are in time, because the representations of both, in so far as they are representations, belong to inner sense. In the same way, whether we consider freedom in the outer or in the inner exercise of choice, its laws, as pure practical laws of reason for free choice as such, must be also the inner determining ground of choice, though we need not always view them in this way.

II.

ON THE IDEA AND NECESSITY OF A METAPHYSIC OF MORALS

I have elsewhere proved that natural science, which deals with objects of outer sense, must have *a priori* principles and that a system of these principles, called a metaphysical science of nature, [214] can and, indeed, must precede physics—that is, its application to particular experience. In order to be universally valid in the strict sense, a principle must be derived from *a priori* grounds. But when physics is concerned only with keeping its propositions free from error, it can accept many principles as universal even though they are based on empirical evidence. Thus Newton assumed on the basis of experience the principle that action and reaction in the influence of bodies on one another are equal, and yet extended it over the whole of material nature, The chemists go still further and base their most universal laws of valence entirely on experience, and still they so trust to the universality and necessity of these laws that they are not concerned about uncovering an error when they undertake experiments with them.

But it is different with moral laws. They are valid as laws only in so far as they can be *seen* to be necessary and to have an *a priori* basis. Indeed, those concepts and judgments about ourselves and our deeds and omissions that can be learned from mere experience are not moral ones at all. And should we let ourselves be led astray into making moral principles out of knowledge drawn from experience, we are exposing ourselves to the grossest and most pernicious errors.

If moral philosophy were merely the doctrine of happiness it would be absurd to seek *a priori* principles for it. For though it may sound plausible to say that reason, even before experience, could see the means for achieving a lasting enjoyment of the true satisfactions of life, all *a priori* teaching about this is either tautological or completely unfounded. Only experience can teach what will bring us satisfaction. Only our natural impulses to food, sex, rest and activity, along with the natural impulses to honour, to increasing our knowledge and so forth (which arise as our natural dispositions develop) can tell us—each in its own way—in what we have to posit that satisfaction; and, in the same way, only experience can teach us the means by which we have to seek it. All specious reasoning *a priori* about this is really nothing other than experience raised by induction [215] to generality, a generality (*secundum principia generalia, non universalia*) which is still so tenuous that each person must be allowed countless exceptions in order to adjust his choice of a way of life to his particular inclinations and his capacity for enjoyment. And so, after all, we acquire prudence only through our own or other people's disappointments.

But it is different with the teachings of morality. They command for everyone, without taking his inclinations into consideration, merely because and in so far as he is free and has practical reason. It is not from observation of ourselves and our animal nature that morality derives the teaching set forth in its laws—not from observation of the ways of the world, of what is done and how people behave (although the German word *Sitten*, like the Latin *mores*, means only manners and customs). On the contrary, reason commands what ought to be done even though no example of this could be found, and it takes no notice of the advantage we can gain by following its commands—advantage that only experience could teach us about. Reason does, indeed, allow us to seek our advantage in every way possible to us, and it can even promise, on the testimony of experience, that we shall probably find it in our interest, on the whole, to follow its commands rather than transgress them, especially if we add prudence to our practice of morality. But the authority of its rules, as *commands*, is not based on these advantages: it uses them (as counsels) only as a counterpoise to the lure of vice, to offset in advance the error of rigged scales in practical judgment and so, in the beginning, to make sure that the weight of pure practical reason's *a priori* grounds will tip the scales.

If, therefore, a system of knowledge *a priori* from mere concepts is called *metaphysics*, then practical philosophy, which has freedom of choice rather than nature as its object, will presuppose and require a metaphysic of morals. In other words, it is a *duty* to have a metaphysic of morals, and everyone has it in himself, though as a rule only in an obscure way; for how could he, without *a priori* principles, believe that he can give universal laws? But just as a metaphysic of nature must also contain principles for applying those universal first principles of nature as such to objects of experience, so a metaphysic of morals [216] cannot dispense with principles of application; and we shall often have to take as our object the particular *nature* of man, which is known only by experience, to show in it the implications of the universal moral principles. But by this we in no way detract from the purity of these principles or cast doubt on their *a priori* source. This is to say, in effect, that a metaphysic of morals cannot be based on anthropology but can be applied to it.

The counterpart of a metaphysic of morals, the other member of the division of practical philosophy in general, would be moral anthropology. But this would concern only the subjective conditions that hinder or help man in *putting into practice* the laws given in a metaphysic of morals. It would deal with the generation, propagation, and strengthening of moral principles (in the education of school children and of the public at large), and other such teachings and precepts based on experience. This cannot be dispensed with, but it must not precede a metaphysic of morals or be mixed with it; for we would then run the risk of bringing forth false or at least indulgent moral laws, mis-

14   [216]

representing, as if it were unattainable, what has not been attained simply because the law has not been seen and presented in its purity (in which its strength consists), or because spurious or impure motives were used for what is in itself dutiful and good. This leaves us with no certain moral principles, either to guide judgment or to discipline the mind in fulfilling our duty; for such precepts must be given *a priori* by pure reason alone.

I have already (in the *Critique of Judgment*) expressed my views on the over-all division of philosophy into theoretical and practical philosophy, which has under it the division discussed in the preceding paragraph, and explained that practical philosophy can be nothing other than moral wisdom. The practical which is supposed to be possible in accordance with laws of nature (and which is the proper concern of art [*Kunst*]) depends for its precepts entirely upon the theory of nature. Only the practical in accordance with laws of freedom can have principles that are independent of any theory; for when we go beyond the workings of nature there is no theory. Hence the practical part of philosophy (as compared with the theoretical part) includes no [217] *technically-practical* doctrine but only *morally-practical doctrine.* And if the term "art" should also be used here to describe the facility of the power of choice to act in accordance with laws of freedom, as contrasted with laws of nature, then we would have to understand by it a kind of art that would make possible a system of freedom comparable to a system of nature—truly a divine art, were we in a position fully to realize, by means of it, what reason prescribes to us and to give effect to its Idea.

III.

ON THE DIVISION OF A METAPHYSIC OF MORALS*

Every legislation contains two elements (whether it prescribes external or inner actions, and whether it prescribes these *a priori* by mere reason or by the choice of another person): *first* a law, which sets forth as objectively necessary the action that ought to take place, *i.e.* which makes the action a duty; *secondly* a motive, which joins a ground determining choice to this action *subjectively* with the thought of the law. Hence the second element consists in this: that the law makes the duty into the motive. The first presents an action as a duty, and this is a merely theoretical recognition of a possible determination of the power of choice, *i.e.* of a practical rule. The second connects the obligation to act in this way with a ground for determining the subject's power of choice as such.

Legislation can therefore be identified by the motives it uses (even if, with regard to the action that it makes a duty, it coincides with another legislation, [218] as when both prescribe external actions). The legislation that makes an action a duty and also makes duty the motive is *ethical*. But the legislation that does not include the motive in the law and so permits a motive other than the Idea of duty itself is

---

* The deduction of the division of a system, *i.e.* the proof that the division is complete and final—which means that the transition from the concept divided to the entire series of the members of the division takes place without a leap (*divisio per saltum*)—is one of the most difficult conditions which the architect of a system has to fulfill. The question of what concept it is whose first division is that into right and wrong (*aut fas aut nefas*) should also give us pause. It is the act of free choice as such. But moral philosophers do not stop to reflect on this, even as the ontologist begins from something and nothing, as if they were the highest concepts, without seeing that they are already members of a division in which the concept divided is still wanting. This concept can be only that of an object as such.

juridical. It is clear that in the case of juridical legislation this motive which is something other than the Idea of duty must be drawn from the pathological determining grounds of choice, the inclinations and aversions, and, among these, from aversion, since the nature of legislation is to necessitate rather than to invite.

The mere conformity or non-conformity of an action with the law, without reference to the motive of the action, is called its *legality* (lawfulness). But that conformity in which the Idea of duty contained in the law is also the motive of the action is called its *morality*.

Duties in accordance with juridical legislation can be only external duties, since this legislation does not require that the inner Idea of the duty be of itself the ground determining the agent's choice; and since it still needs a motive appropriate to the law, it can connect only external motives with the law. But ethical legislation, while it makes inner actions duties as well, does not exclude external actions: it is concerned with all duties in so far as they are duties. But just because ethical legislation includes in its law the inner motive of the action (the Idea of duty), which must not be considered in outer legislation, it cannot be outer *legislation* (not even that of a divine will). It does, however, admit into itself duties which are based on another (outer) legislation, by making them, *as duties*, motives in ethical legislation.

From this it can be seen that all duties, merely because they are duties, belong to ethics. But it does not follow that their legislation is always contained in ethics: in the case of many duties it lies outside ethics. Thus ethics commands that I fulfill a contract I have entered into, even if the other party could not compel me to do it. But it accepts the law (*pacta sunt servanda*) and the duty corresponding to it

17

from the doctrine of Law, as [219] already given there. Accordingly, the legislation that promises agreed to must be kept does not lie in ethics but rather in *ius*. All that ethics teaches about it is that if the motive which juridical legislation connects with that duty—external compulsion—is let go, the Idea of duty by itself must be the sufficient motive. For if this were not the case—were the legislation itself not juridical and the duty springing from it not really a juridical duty (as distinguished from a duty of virtue)— then faithful performance (of the promises made in a contract) would be put in the same class with acts of benevolence and the obligation to them. And this must not happen. To keep one's promises is no duty of virtue but a juridical duty, one which we can be compelled to fulfill. But it is still a virtuous action (a proof of virtue) to keep our promises even when we need not *worry* about compulsion. Hence what distinguishes the doctrine of Law from the doctrine of virtue is not so much their different duties as rather the different kinds of legislation which connect one or the other motive with the law.

Ethical legislation *cannot* be external (even if all the duties in question are external ones): juridical legislation, like the duties, can be external. Thus it is an external duty to keep the promises made in a contract; but the command to do this merely because it is a duty and without regard for any other motive belongs only to *inner* legislation. So the reason for assigning an obligation to ethics is not that the duty is of a particular kind (a particular kind of action to which we are obligated)—for there are external duties in ethics as well as in Law—but rather that the legislation is inner legislation and there can be no external lawgiver. Thus duties of benevolence, although they are external duties (obligations to external actions), belong to ethics, because only inner legislation can enjoin them.—Ethics does have its special duties as well (for example, duties to oneself), but it also has duties in common with Law. What ethics does not have in common with Law is only the kind of *obligation* [to these duties]. For the characteristic property of ethical legislation is that it commands us to perform actions merely because they are duties and to make the principle of duty itself the sufficient motive of our choice. [220] Thus there are, indeed, many *directly ethical* duties, but inner legislation makes all other duties indirectly ethical.

IV.

CONCEPTS PRELIMINARY TO THE METAPHYSIC OF MORALS

(*Philosophia practica universalis*)

The concept of *freedom* is a pure rational concept, which is therefore transcendent for theoretical philosophy: because the concept of freedom is such that no example adequate to it can ever be given in any possible experience, freedom is not an object of our possible theoretical knowledge. For speculative reason the concept of freedom can have no validity as a constitutive principle but solely as a regulative and, indeed, merely negative principle. But in reason's practical use the concept of freedom proves its reality through practical principles which, as laws of a causality of pure reason which is independent of all empirical conditions (of sensibility as such), determine choice and prove the existence in us of a pure will in which moral concepts and laws have their source.

On practical reason's positive concept of freedom there are based unconditioned practical laws called *moral* laws. But since our power of choice is sensuously affected and so does not of itself conform with the pure will but often opposes it, in relation to us these moral laws are *imperatives* (commands or prohibitions) and, indeed, categorical (unconditioned) imperatives. As such they are distinguished from technical imperatives (precepts of art [*Kunstvorschriften*]), which are always merely conditioned commands. According to categorical imperatives certain actions are *permissible* or *impermissible*, *i.e.* morally possible or impossible, while some of these actions or their contraries are morally necessary, *i.e.* obligatory. From these arises the concept of a duty whose fulfillment or transgression is connected with pleasure or pain of a special kind (of moral *feeling*). But in discussing practical laws of reason we do not take this feeling into account, since it does not concern the *ground* of these laws but only the subjective *effect* which they have on our mind when they determine our power of choice. And this effect can differ from one subject to the next without objectively (that is, in the judgment of reason) adding to or detracting from the validity or influence of these laws. [221]

The following concepts are common to both parts of the Metaphysic of Morals.

Obligation is the necessity of a free action under a categorical imperative.

An imperative is a practical rule which *makes* necessary an action that is in itself contingent. An imperative differs from a practical law in that a law, when it states that an action is necessary, takes no account of whether the action is also *subjectively* necessary on the agent's part (he could be a holy being) or whether the action is in itself contingent (as in the case of man). If the action is subjectively necessary there is no imperative. Hence an imperative is a rule which makes a subjectively contingent action necessary and thus shows that the

[221]

agent is one who must be *necessitated* to conform with this rule.—The categorical (unconditioned) imperative views the action as objectively necessary and necessitates the agent to it immediately, by the mere thought of the action itself (*i.e.* of its form), and not mediately, by the thought of an *end* to be attained by the action. The only practical doctrine which can bring forth instances of such imperatives is the one that lays down obligation (the doctrine of morality). All other imperatives are *technical* imperatives; they are, one and all, conditioned. The *ground* of the possibility of categorical imperatives is this: that they are based simply on the *freedom* of the power of choice, not on any other characteristic of choice (by which it can be subjected to a purpose).

An action which is not contrary to obligation is *permissible* (*licitum*); and this freedom, which is not limited by any opposing imperative, is called a moral title (*facultas moralis*). From this the definition of the *impermissible* (*illicitum*) is self-evident.

A *duty* is an action to which we are obligated. It is, accordingly, the matter of obligation, and we can be obligated in different ways to one and the same duty (that is, to one and the same action which is a duty).

In so far as the categorical imperative asserts an obligation with respect to certain actions, it is a morally-practical [222] *law*. But since obligation includes *necessitation* as well as the practical necessity that a law as such expresses, a categorical imperative is a law which either commands or prohibits; it sets forth as a duty the commission or omission of an action. An action that is neither commanded nor forbidden is merely *permissible*, since there is no law to limit one's freedom (moral title) to perform it, and so no duty with regard to the action.

An action of this kind is called morally indifferent (*indifferens, adiaphoron, res merae facultatis*). The question can be raised *whether there are* morally indifferent actions and, if so, whether we must admit permissive law (*lex permissiva*), in addition to commands and prohibitions (*lex praeceptiva, lex mandati* and *lex prohibitiva, lex vetiti*), in order to account for this moral title to act or refrain from acting as one pleases. In that case, the action to which the moral title refers would not be indifferent (*adiaphoron*) in every case; for according to moral laws, no special law is needed for an action that is always indifferent.

An action is called a *deed* in so far as it comes under obligatory laws and hence in so far as it is referred to the freedom of the agent's power of choice. The agent is considered the *author* of the effects of his deed, and these, along with the action itself, can be *imputed* to him if, before he acts, he knows the law by virtue of which they come under an obligation.

A *person* is a subject whose actions can be *imputed* to him. *Moral* personality is thus the freedom of a rational being under moral laws. (Psychological personality is merely the power to become conscious of one's self-identity at different times and under the different conditions of one's existence.) From this it follows that a person is subject to no other laws than those which he (either alone or at least along with others) gives himself.

A *thing* is something that is not susceptible of imputation. Thus any object of free choice which itself lacks freedom is called a thing (*res corporalis*).

A deed is *right* or *wrong* (*rectum aut minus rectum*) when it conforms with duty or is contrary to duty (*factum licitum aut* [223] *illicitum*); the duty itself, so far as its content or its source is concerned, may be of any kind whatsoever. A deed contrary to duty is called a *transgression* (*reatus*).

An *unintentional* transgression which can still be imputed to the agent is called a mere *fault* (*culpa*). An *intentional* transgression (*i.e.* one which the agent knows is a transgression) is called a *crime* (*dolus*). What is right in accordance with external laws is called *just* (*iustum*): what is wrong, unjust (*iniustum*).

A *conflict of duties* (*collisio officiorum s. obligationum*) would be a relation of duties in which one of them would annul the other (wholly or in part).—But a *conflict of duties* and obligations is inconceivable (*obligationes non colliduntur*). For the concepts of duty and obligation as such express the objective practical *necessity* of certain actions, and two conflicting rules cannot both be necessary at the same time: if it is our duty to act according to one of these rules, then to act according to the opposite one is not our duty and is even contrary to duty. But there can, it is true, be two *grounds* of obligation (*rationes obligandi*) both present in one agent and in the rule he lays down for himself. In this case one or the other of these grounds is not sufficient to oblige him (*rationes obligandi non obligantes*) and is therefore not a duty.—When two such grounds conflict with each other, practical philosophy says, not that the stronger obligation takes precedence (*fortior obligatio vincit*), but that the stronger *ground of obligation* prevails (*fortior obligandi ratio vincit*).

Obligatory laws that can be given in outer legislation are called *external* laws (*leges externae*) in general. If their power to obligate can be recognized *a priori* by reason, even apart from outer legislation, they are *natural* external laws. But if actual outer legislation is needed to make them obligatory (and so to make them laws), they are called *positive* laws. We can therefore conceive an outer legislation which would contain only positive laws; but this would still presuppose a natural law establishing the authority of the legislator (*i.e.* his moral title to obligate others by his mere act of choice). [224]

The principle that makes certain actions duties is a practical law. The rule that the agent himself makes his principle on subjective grounds is called his *maxim*. Thus different men can have quite different maxims with regard to the same law.

The categorical imperative, which as such only expresses what obligation is, reads: act according to a maxim which can, at the same time, be valid as a universal law.—You must, therefore, begin by looking at the subjective principle of your action. But to know whether this principle is also objectively valid, your reason must subject it to the test of conceiving yourself as giving universal law through this principle. If your maxim qualifies for a giving of universal law, then it is objectively valid.

The simplicity of this law, compared with its great and manifold implications, must seem astonishing at first. So must its imperious authority, in view of the fact that the law, despite its authority, carries no perceptible motive with it. But while we are wondering at the power of our reason to determine choice by the mere Idea that our maxim qualifies for the *universality* of a practical law, we realize that these same practical (moral) laws first make known and establish beyond all doubt a property of our power of choice—its freedom—which speculative reason would never have hit upon by itself, either from *a priori* grounds or by any experience whatsoever, and which, when it is attained, can never be proved possible on theoretical grounds. Then we are less astonished to find that these laws, like mathematical postulates, are *indemonstrable* and yet *apodictic,* and at the same time to see a whole field of practical knowledge open before us, where theoretical reason, with this same Idea of freedom—indeed with all its other Ideas of the supersensible—must find everything closed tight against it.—The conformity of an action with the law of duty is its *legality (legalitas):* the conformity of the maxim of the action with the law is the *morality* (*moralitas*) of the action. A *maxim* is the *subjective* principle of action, the principle which the subject himself makes his rule (how he chooses to act). The principle of duty, on the other hand, is the principle that reason prescribes to him absolutely and so objectively (how he *ought* to act). [225]

The first principle of morality is, therefore: act according to a maxim which can, at the same time, be valid as universal law.—Any maxim which does not so qualify is contrary to morality.

Laws proceed from the will—maxims from the power of choice. In man the power of choice is a power of free choice. The will, which does not look to anything beyond the law itself, cannot be called either free or unfree, since it does not look to actions but rather, in an immediate way, to legislating for the maxims of actions (and so to practical reason itself). Thus the will functions with absolute necessity and itself *admits of* no necessitation. It is, therefore, only the power of choice that can be called *free.*

Some have tried to define freedom of choice as the power to choose between the alternatives of acting with or against the law (*libertas indifferentiae*). But freedom of choice cannot be defined in this way, although the power of choice as *phenomenon* gives frequent examples of this in experience. For we know freedom (as it is first made knowable to us through the moral law) only as a *negative* property in us: the property of not being *necessitated* to act by any sensuous determining ground. But we cannot explain *theoretically* freedom in its positive aspect, as it *exercises necessitation* on the sensuous power of choice—that is, freedom as *noumenon*, as the power of man viewed merely as an intelligent being. We can see only this: that while our experience of man as a *sensible being* shows that he can choose to act *against* the law as well as *in conformity with* it, his freedom as an *intelligible being* cannot be *defined* by this, since appearances cannot explain a supersensible object (like free choice); and that freedom cannot be located in the rational agent's ability to choose what is opposed to his (legislating) reason, even if experience proves often enough that this happens (though we still cannot conceive the possibility of it).—For it is one thing to admit this proposition (on the basis of experience) and another thing to make it into the *principle that defines* the concept of free choice and serves as the universal criterion for distinguishing it (from *arbitrio bruto s. servo*). Merely to admit a proposition on the basis of experience [226] is not to say that the characteristic so admitted belongs *necessarily* to the concept, but to define the concept in terms of the characteristic does imply this.—Only freedom with regard to the inner legislation of reason is really a power: the possibility of deviating from legislative reason is a lack of power. How, then, can this possibility be used to define freedom? Such a definition would add to the practical concept the *exercise* of it, as this is taught by experience; it would be a hybrid definition (*definitio hybrida*) which presents the concept in a false light.

A (morally-practical) *law* is a proposition that contains a categorical imperative (command). He who commands (*imperans*) through a law is the *legislator*. He is the *author* (*auctor*) of the obligation which accompanies the law, but not always the author of the law. If he is the author of the law, it is a positive (contingent) and arbitrary law. The law which obligates us *a priori* and unconditionally by our own reason can also be expressed as proceeding from the will of a supreme legislator, *i.e.* one who has only rights and no duties (and so as from the divine will). But this signifies only the Idea of a moral being whose will is law for everyone; it does not mean that this being is the author of the law.

Imputation (*imputatio*) in the moral sense is the *judgment* by which one is considered the author (*causa libera*) of an action that comes under laws and is thus called a *deed* (*factum*). When imputation also carries with it the legal consequences of this action, it is called an imputation that has legal effect (*imputatio iudiciaria s. valida*); otherwise it is merely an *evaluating* imputation (*imputatio diiudicatoria*). The (natural or moral) person who has the moral title to impute the legal effects of an action is called the *judge* or court (*iudex s. forum*).

If someone does *more* in the way of duty than the law can compel him to do, his action is *meritorious* (*meritum*). If he does only the *exact* thing required by the law, he does what is *due* (*debitum*). Finally, if he does *less* than the law requires, this is moral *guilt* (*demeritum*). The *legal* effect of guilt is *punishment* (*poena*); that of a meritorious deed is *reward* (*praemium*), (assuming that the reward, promised in the law, was the inducement). The [227] conformity of conduct with what is due has no legal effect.—There is no such thing as a *legal relation* of *benevolent requital* (*remuneratio s. respensio benefica*) to a deed.

The good or bad effects of a due action, like the effects following from the omission of a meritorious action, cannot be imputed to the subject (*modus imputationis tollens*).

The good effects of a meritorious action, like the bad effects of an unlawful action, can be imputed to the subject (*modus imputationis ponens*).

The *subjective degree of responsibility* (*imputabilitas*) for an action must be judged according to the magnitude of the obstacles which had to be surmounted in the action.—In proportion as the natural obstacles (of sensibility) are greater and the moral obstacle (of duty) is smaller, so much the more is a good action accounted to one's merit, as when, for example, with considerable self-sacrifice I rescue a total stranger from great distress.

Conversely, in proportion as the natural obstacle is smaller and the moral obstacle based on duty is greater, so much the more guilt is imputed to me for a transgression of duty.—Hence the agent's state of mind—whether he did the deed in a state of agitation or with calm deliberation—makes a difference in the imputation, a difference that has [legal] effects.

METAPHYSICAL FIRST PRINCIPLES OF THE DOCTRINE OF VIRTUE

Part II of

The Metaphysic of Morals

PREFACE
to the
Doctrine of Virtue

A *philosophy* of any subject (a system of rational knowledge from concepts) requires a system of *pure rational* concepts which are independent of all conditions of intuition, *i.e.* a *metaphysics*.—The question is only whether every *practical* philosophy, as a doctrine of duties—and so, too, the *doctrine of virtue* (ethics)—needs *metaphysical first principles* in order that it may be set forth as a true science (systematically) and not merely as an aggregate of precepts sought out one by one (fragmentarily).—No one would question whether the pure doctrine of Law needs metaphysical first principles; for the doctrine of Law, which abstracts from all *ends* as the matter of choice, deals only with the *formal condition* of a power of choice that is limited in external relations by laws of freedom. This doctrine of duties is, accordingly, a *mere doctrine of science (doctrina scientiae).**

* An *authority on practical philosophy* is not thereby a *practical philosopher*. A practical philosopher is one who makes the *final end of reason* the principle *of his own actions* and couples with this the knowledge required. Since this knowledge is directed to action it need not be spun into the finest threads of metaphysics, unless it should happen to concern a juridical duty; then the *Mine* and *Thine* must be determined on the scales of justice with quasi-mathematical precision, according to the principle that action and reaction are equal. But so long as this knowledge concerns a mere duty of virtue, this is not

But so far as the philosophy now in question (the doctrine of virtue) is concerned, it seems directly contrary to the Idea of it to go all the way back to *metaphysical first principles* [375] in order to make the concept of duty, though purified of everything empirical (every feeling), the motive. For what kind of a concept can we form, of such power and herculean strength that it could subdue the vice-breeding inclinations, if virtue has to borrow its weapons from the arsenal of metaphysics, a speculative subject that few people know how to handle? Thus all doctrine of virtue—in the lecture rooms, from the pulpits, or in popular books—will become ridiculous if it is decked out in scraps of metaphysics. —But it is not useless, much less ridiculous, to trace the first grounds of the doctrine of virtue back to metaphysics; for someone must still, as a philosopher, go to the first grounds of this concept of duty, since otherwise we can expect neither certitude nor purity in any part of the doctrine of virtue. I grant that a popular teacher can be content to rely on a certain *feeling* which, because of the results expected from it, is called *moral*, in so far as he insists that the following principle be taken to heart, as the touchstone for deciding whether something is a duty of virtue or not: "could a maxim such as yours harmonize with itself if everyone, in every case, made it a universal law?" But if it were mere feeling that made even the use of this touchstone a duty, then this duty would not

---

necessary. For being a practical philosopher does not depend merely on knowing what it is one's duty to do (by reason of the ends which all men naturally have it is easy to state what one's duty is). It depends primarily on the inner principle of the will: that the thought of this duty be also the *motive* of actions. The man who joins this principle of wisdom with his knowledge can be called a *practical philosopher*.

be dictated by reason; it would be accepted as a duty merely instinctively, and so blindly.

But in fact no moral principle is based, as people sometimes suppose, on any *feeling* whatsoever. Any such principle is really an obscurely thought *metaphysics*, which is inherent in the structure of every man's reason, as any teacher will readily grant if he experiments in questioning his pupil *socratically* about the imperative of duty and its application to moral judgment of his actions. —The way the teacher *talks* about duty (his technique) need not always be metaphysical nor his terms scholastic, unless he wants to educate his pupil as a philosopher. But the *thought* must go all the way back to the elements of metaphysics, for without these the doctrine of virtue can have neither certitude nor purity nor even motive power.

If we depart from this principle and begin with pathological or pure aesthetic or even moral *feeling* (the subjectively-practical rather than the objective) —if, in other words, we try to determine duties by beginning with the matter of the will, the *end*, rather than with the form of the will, the *law*, [376] as our basis—then we shall indeed have no *metaphysical first principles* of the doctrine of virtue; for feeling, no matter by what it is aroused, always belongs to the order of *nature*. —But then the doctrine of virtue will be corrupted at its very source, and so corrupted alike in the schools, the lecture rooms, *etc.* For the kind of motive that leads one to adopt a good intention (that of fulfilling every duty) is not irrevelant. —Hence, no matter how much *metaphysics* may disgust the alleged teachers of wisdom who discourse on duty as *oracles* or men of *genius*, these same people who turn up their noses at metaphysics still have an essential duty to go back to the metaphysical first principles of the doctrine of virtue and, before they teach, to become pupils in their own classrooms.

* * *

After all these explanations that the principle of duty is derived from pure reason, it is remarkable how *hedonism* can survive, though now in a form that makes a certain *moral* happiness, whose causes are not empirical (a self-contradictory concept), the end.—It happens in this way. When the reflective man has overcome the incentives to vice and is conscious of having done his often painful duty, he finds himself in a state which could well be called happiness, a state of contentment and peace of soul in which virtue is its own reward. —Now the *eudaemonist* says: this delight or happiness is really his motive for acting virtuously. The concept of duty does not determine his will *immediately;* he is moved to do his duty only *through the medium of* the happiness he foresees. —But if he can expect this reward of virtue only from consciousness of having done his duty, then obviously, consciousness of having done his duty must come first. In other words, he must find himself under obligation to do his duty before he thinks of the fact that happiness will result from doing it and without thinking of this. The eudaemonist's *etiology* involves him in a vicious circle: he can hope to be *happy* (or inwardly blissful) only if he is conscious of having done his duty, but he can be moved to do his duty only if he foresees that it will make him happy. —But [377] there is also a *contradiction* in this sophistry. For he ought to do his duty on *moral* grounds or without first asking what effect this will have on his happiness: yet he can recognize that something is his duty only on *pathological* grounds, by whether he can count on gaining happiness by doing that thing. And these two are diametrically opposed to each other.

In another place (the *Berlinische Monatsschrift*) I have, I think, reduced the distinction between *pathological* and *moral pleasure* to its simplest terms: the pleasure that must precede our obedience to the law in order for us to act in conformity with the law is pathological, and our conduct then follows the *order of nature;* but the pleasure that we can feel only after [having determined to obey] the law is in the *moral order.*—If we fail to observe this distinction, and take as our basic principle *eudaemonism* (the happiness principle) instead of *eleutheronomy* (the freedom principle of inner legislation), we effect the *euthanasia* (painless death) of all morals.

The cause of these errors is simply this: people who are used to merely physiological explanations cannot get it into their heads that there is a categorical imperative from which moral laws proceed dictatorially, even though they feel themselves compelled irresistibly by it. These people are dedicated to the omnipotence of theoretical reason, and the discomfort they feel at not being able to *explain* what lies entirely beyond the sphere of physiological explanation (*freedom* of choice) provokes them to a general *call to arms*, as it were, to withstand that Idea, no matter how exalting this very prerogative of man—his capacity for such an *Idea*—may be. For they grant, here too, the proud claims of theoretical reason, which feels its power so strong in other fields. And so now, and perhaps for a while longer, they assail the moral concept of freedom and, wherever possible, make it suspect; but in the end they must give way. [378]

INTRODUCTION
to the
Doctrine of Virtue

In ancient times "ethics" meant *moral philosophy* (*philosophia moralis*) in general, which was also called the *doctrine of duties*. Later on it seemed better to reserve the name "ethics" for one part of moral philosophy, for the doctrine of those duties that do not come under external laws (in German, the name *doctrine of virtue* was thought appropriate for this). Accordingly the system of the doctrine of duties in general is now divided into the system of the *doctrine of Law* (*ius*), which deals with duties that can be enjoined by external laws, and the system of the *doctrine of virtue* (*ethica*), which treats of duties that cannot be so prescribed; and this division may stand.

I.

EXPOSITION OF THE CONCEPT OF A DOCTRINE OF VIRTUE

The *concept of duty* as such is the notion of a *necessitation* (constraint) of *free* choice by the law; this constraint may be either *external* compulsion or *self*-constraint.[3] The moral *imperative* announces this constraint by its categorical dictum (the unconditioned *Ought*). Hence the constraint does not refer to rational beings as such (there might be *holy* ones) but rather to *men, natural beings* endowed with reason who are unholy enough that pleasure can induce them to transgress the moral law, even though they recognize its authority. And when they do obey the law, they do it *reluctantly* (in the face of opposition from their inclinations), and so under *constraint.** —But since man is still a *free* (moral) [379] being, when the concept of duty concerns the inner determination of his choice (the motive), the constraint which duty contains can be only *self-constraint* (by the mere thought of the law); for only so can freedom of choice be reconciled with that *necessitation* (even if it be external). Hence in this case the concept of duty will be an ethical one.

The impulses of nature, accordingly, are *obstacles* within man's mind to his observance of duty and forces (sometimes powerful ones) struggling against it. Man must, therefore, judge that he is able to stand up to them and subdue them by reason—not at some time in the future but at once (the moment he thinks of duty): he must judge that he *can* do what the law commands unconditionally that he *ought* to do.

Now the power and deliberate resolve to withstand a strong but unjust opponent is *fortitude* (*fortitudo*); and

---

* Yet if man looks at himself objectively—under the aspect of *humanity* in his own person, as his pure practical reason determines him to do—he finds that, *as a moral being*, he is also holy enough to transgress the inner law *reluctantly;* for there is no man so depraved as not to feel an opposition to this transgression and an abhorrence of himself on account of which he has to constrain himself [to violate the law]. —Now it is impossible to explain the phenomenon that at this parting of the ways (where the beautiful fable pictures Hercules between virtue and sensual pleasure) man shows more propensity to listen to his inclinations than to the law. For we can explain what happens only by deriving the event from a cause in accordance with laws of nature, and in trying to explain the act of choice we would not be thinking of it as free. —But it is this mutual and opposing self-constraint and the inevitability of it that makes known the inexplicable property of *freedom* itself.

[379]   37

fortitude in relation to the forces opposing a moral attitude of will *in us* is <u>virtue</u> (*virtus, fortitudo moralis*). So the part of the general doctrine of duties that brings inner, rather than outer, freedom under laws is a *doctrine of virtue*.

The doctrine of Law deals only with the *formal* condition of outer freedom (the consistency of outer freedom with itself if its maxim were made universal law)—that is, with <u>Law</u>. But ethics goes beyond this and provides a *matter* (an object of free choice), an <u>end</u> of pure reason which it presents also as an objectively necessary end, *i.e.* an end which, so far as men are concerned, it is a duty to have. —For since the sensuous inclinations tempt us to ends (as the matter of choice) which may be contrary to duty, |380| legislative reason can check their influence only by another end, a moral end set up against the ends of inclination, which must therefore by given *a priori*, independently of the inclinations.

An *end* is an object of the power of choice (of a rational being), through the thought of which choice is determined to an action to produce this object. —Now another person can indeed compel me to perform actions which are means to his end, but he cannot compel me *to have an end;* only I myself can make something my end. —But the notion that I am under obligation to take as my end something that lies in the concepts of practical reason, and so to have a material determining ground of choice beyond the formal one that Law contains, would be the concept of an *end which is in itself a duty*. The doctrine of this end would not belong to the doctrine of Law but rather to ethics, since the concept of *self-constraint* in accordance with moral laws belongs only to ethics.

For this reason ethics can also be defined as the system of the *ends* of pure practical reason. —Ends and duties [to which we can be compelled by others] differentiate the two divisions of moral philosophy in general. That ethics contains duties which others cannot compel us (by natural means) to fulfill is merely the consequence of its being a doctrine of *ends;* for compulsion to have or to adopt ends is self-contradictory.

That ethics is a *doctrine of virtue* (*doctrina officiorum virtutis*—[doctrine of the offices of virtue]) follows from the above definition of virtue when we connect it with the kind of obligation proper to ethics. —Determination to an *end* is the only determination of choice which in its very concept excludes the possibility of compulsion *through natural means* by another's *act of choice.* Another can indeed *compel* me to do something that is not my end (but only a means to his end), but he cannot compel me *to make it my end.* To have an end that I have not myself made an end would be a self-contradiction—an act of freedom which is still not free. —But it is no contradiction that I myself set an end which is also a duty, since I constrain myself to it and this is altogether [381] consistent with freedom.* —But how is such an end possible? That is the question now. For the fact that the concept of a thing is possible (contains no contradiction) is not yet sufficient

---

* The less a man can be compelled by natural means and the more he can be constrained morally (through the mere thought of the law), so much the more free he is. —Suppose, for example, a man so firm of purpose and strong of soul that he cannot be dissuaded from a pleasure he intends to have, no matter how others may reason with him about the harm he will do himself by it. If such a man gives up his plan immediately, though reluctantly, at the thought that it would cause him to omit one of his duties as an official or neglect a sick father, he proves his freedom in the highest degree by being unable to resist the call of duty.

ground for assuming the possibility of the thing itself (the objective reality of the concept).

II.

EXPOSITION OF THE CONCEPT OF AN END WHICH
IS AT THE SAME TIME A DUTY

We can conceive the relation of end and duty in two ways: we can begin with the end and seek out the *maxim* of dutiful actions, or we can begin with this maxim and seek out the *end* which is also a duty. —The *doctrine of Law* takes the first way. It leaves it to each man's free choice to decide what end he wants to adopt for his action; but it determines *a priori* the maxim of this action, namely, that the freedom of the agent can co-exist with the freedom of every other in accordance with a universal law.

Ethics takes the opposite way. It cannot begin with the ends a man may set for himself and then prescribe, on this basis, the maxim he ought to adopt—that is, his duty. For in that case the grounds of the maxim would be empirical, and such grounds yield no concept of duty, since this concept (the categorical Ought) has its roots in pure reason alone. Consequently, if maxims had to be adopted on the basis of such ends (all of which are self-seeking), we could not really speak of the concept of duty. —Hence in ethics the *concept of duty* will lead to ends, and *maxims* concerning the ends we *ought* to adopt must be established according to moral principles. [382]

Setting aside the question of what sort of end is in itself a duty and how such an end is possible, we have here only to show that a duty of this kind is called a *"duty of virtue"* and why it is called this.

To every duty there corresponds *one* right in the sense of a *moral title* (*facultas moralis generatim*); but only a

particular kind of duty, *juridical duty*, implies corresponding *rights* of other people to exercise compulsion (*facultas
iuridica*). —In the same way, every ethical *obligation* implies the concept of virtue, but not all ethical duties are
thereby duties of virtue. Those duties which concern, not
so much a certain end (matter, object of choice), but what
is merely *formal* in the moral determination of the will (*e.g.*
that the due action should also be done *from the motive of
duty*), are not duties of virtue. Only an *end which is also a
duty* can be called a <u>duty of virtue</u>. For this reason there
can be many duties of virtue (and also many different
virtues), while there is only one formal element of moral
choice (one virtuous attitude of will), which is, however,
valid for all actions.

What essentially distinguishes a duty of virtue from a
juridical duty is the fact that external compulsion to a
juridical duty is morally possible, whereas a duty of virtue is
based only on free self-constraint. —For finite *holy* beings
(who can never be tempted to transgress duty) there is no
doctrine of virtue but merely a doctrine of morality, since
morality is an autonomy of practical reason while virtue is
also an *autocracy* of practical reason. Virtue contains, in
other words, consciousness of the *power* to master one's
inclinations when they rebel against the law—a consciousness which, though not immediately given, is yet rightly de-
duced from the moral categorical imperative. Thus human
morality in its highest stages can still be nothing more than
virtue, not even if it were entirely pure (quite free from
the influence of any motive other than duty), as when it is
often personified poetically in the *Sage*, as an ideal (to
which we must continually approximate).

But virtue cannot be defined and valued as a mere *aptitude* or (as the prize-essay of Cochius, the court-chaplain,

puts it[4]) a long-standing *habit* of morally good actions, acquired by practice. For unless this aptitude results from considered, firm, and continually purified principles, then, like any other [383] mechanism of technically-practical reason, it is neither armed for all situations nor adequately insured against the changes that new temptations could bring about.

Note

Virtue (= +a) is opposed to *negative lack of virtue* (moral weakness = O) as its *logical opposite* (*contradictorie oppositum*); but it is opposed to vice = −a) as its *real opposite* (*contrarie s. realiter oppositum*). And it is not only unnecessary but even improper to ask whether great *crimes* might not evidence more strength of soul than do great *virtues*. For by strength of soul we mean the strength of resolution in a man as a being endowed with freedom— hence his strength in so far as he is in control of himself (in his senses) and so in the *state of health* proper to a man. But great crimes are paroxysms, the sight of which makes a man shudder if he is sound of soul. The question would therefore come to something like this: whether a man in a fit of madness could have more physical strength than when he is sane. And we can admit this without attributing more strength of soul to him, if by soul we mean the life principle of man in the free use of his powers; for since a madman's strength, having its source merely in the force of inclinations which *weaken* his reason, manifests no strength of soul, the above question would amount to much the same thing as whether a man could show more strength when he is sick than when he is healthy. This we can straightway deny, since health consists in the balance of all man's bodily powers and sickness is a weakening in the system of these powers; and it is only by reference to this system that we can judge absolute health.

ON THE GROUND FOR CONCEIVING AN END WHICH
IS AT THE SAME TIME A DUTY

An *end* is an *object* of free choice, the thought of which determines the power of choice to an action by which the object is produced. [384] Every action, therefore, has its end; and since no one can have an end without *himself* making the object of choice into an end, it follows that the adoption of any end of action whatsoever is an act of *freedom* on the agent's part, not an operation of *nature*. But if this act which determines an end is a practical principle that prescribes the end itself (and therefore commands unconditionally), not the means (and so not conditionally), it is a categorical imperative of pure practical reason.[5] It is, therefore, an imperative which connects a *concept of duty* with that of an end as such.

Now there must be such an end and a categorical imperative corresponding to it. For since there are free actions there must also be ends to which, as their object, these actions are directed. But among these ends there must also be some that are at the same time (that is, by their concept) duties. —For were there no such ends, then all ends would be valid for practical reason only as means to other ends; and since there can be no action without an end, a *categorical* imperative would be impossible. And this would do away with all moral philosophy.

Thus we are not speaking here of the ends man sets for himself according to the sensuous impulses of his nature, but of the objects of free choice under its laws—objects man *ought to adopt* as ends. The study of the former type of ends can be called the technical (subjective) doctrine of ends: it is really the pragmatic doctrine of ends, comprising the rules of prudence in the choice of one's ends. The study of the latter type of ends, however, must be called the moral (objective) doctrine of ends. But this distinction is superfluous here, since the very concept of moral philosphy already distinguishes it clearly from the doctrine of nature (in this case anthropology) by the fact that anthropology is based on empirical principles, while the moral doctrine of ends, which treats of duties, is based on principles given *a priori* in pure practical reason.

IV.
WHAT ENDS ARE ALSO DUTIES?

They are *one's own perfection* and the *happiness of others*.

We cannot interchange perfection and happiness here. In other words, *one's own happiness* and the *perfection of other men* cannot be made into obligatory ends of the same person. [385]

Since every man (by virtue of his *natural* impulses) has *his own happiness* as his end, it would be contradictory to consider this an obligatory end. What we will inevitably and spontaneously does not come under the concept of *duty*, which is *necessitation* to an end we adopt reluctantly. Hence it is contradictory to say that we are *under obligation* to promote our own happiness to the best of our ability.

In the same way, it is contradictory to say that I make another person's *perfection* my end and consider myself obligated to promote this. For the *perfection* of another man, as a person, consists precisely in *his own* power to adopt his end in accordance with his own concept of duty;

44   [385]

and it is self-contradictory to demand that I do (make it my duty to do) what only the other person himself can do.

v.

CLARIFICATION OF THESE TWO CONCEPTS

A. One's Own Perfection

The word *"perfection"* is open to many misinterpretations. Perfection is sometimes understood as a concept belonging to transcendental philosophy—the concept of the *totality* of the manifold which, taken together, constitutes a thing. Then again, in so far as it belongs to *teleology* it is taken to mean the adequacy of a thing's qualities to an *end*. Perfection in the first sense could be called *quantitative* (material) perfection: in the second, *qualitative* (formal) perfection. The quantitative perfection of a thing can be only one (for the totality of what belongs to a thing is one). But one thing can have a number of qualitative perfections, and it is really qualitative perfection that we are discussing here.

When we say that man has a duty to take as his end the perfection characteristic of man as such (of humanity, really), we must locate perfection in what man can bring into being by his actions, not in the mere gifts he receives from nature; for otherwise it would not be a duty to make perfection an end. This duty must [386] therefore be the *cultivation* of one's *powers* (or natural capacities), the highest of which is *understanding*, the power of concepts and so too of those concepts that belong to duty. At the same time this duty includes the cultivation of one's *will* (moral attitude) to fulfill every duty as such. 1) Man has a duty of striving to raise himself from the crude state of his nature, from his animality (*quoad actum*[6]) and to realize ever more fully in himself the humanity by which he alone is capable of setting ends: it is his duty to diminish his ignorance by education and to correct his errors. And it is not merely technically-practical reason that *counsels* him to acquire skill as a means to his further aims (of art [*Kunst*]): morally-practical reason *commands* it absolutely and makes this end his duty, that he may be worthy of the humanity in him. 2) Man has a duty of cultivating his *will* to the purest attitude of virtue, in which the law is the motive as well as the norm for his actions and he obeys it from duty. This is the duty of striving for inner morally-practical perfection. Since this perfection is a feeling of the influence which the legislative will within man exercises on his power of acting in accordance with this will, it is called *moral feeling*—a special *sense* (*sensus moralis*), as it were. It is true that moral sense is often misused in a visionary way, as if (like Socrates' genius) it could precede or even dispense with reason's judgment. Yet it is a moral perfection, by which one makes each particular obligatory end one's object.

B. *The Happiness of Others*

By a tendency of his nature man inevitably wants and seeks his own happiness, *i.e.* contentment with his state along with the assurance that it will last; and for this reason one's own happiness is not an obligatory end. —Some people, however, invent a distinction between moral happiness, which they define as contentment with our own person and moral conduct and so with what we *do*, and natural happiness, which is satisfaction with what nature bestows and so with what we *enjoy* as a gift from without. (I refrain here from censuring a misuse of the word "happiness" which already involves a contradiction.) It must therefore be noted that the feeling of moral happiness belongs only under the [387] preceding heading of perfection; for the man who is said to be happy in the mere consciousness of his integrity already possesses the perfection defined there as the end which it is also his duty to have.

When it comes to my pursuit of happiness as an obligatory end, this must therefore be the happiness of *other* men, *whose* (permissible) *ends I thus make my own ends as well*. It is for them to decide what things they consider elements in their happiness; but I am entitled to refuse some of these things if I disagree with their judgments, so long as the other has no right to demand a thing from me as his due. But time and again an alleged *obligation* to attend to *my own* (natural) happiness is set up in competition with this end, and my natural and merely subjective end is thus made a duty (an obligatory end). Since this is used as a specious objection to the division of duties made above (in IV), it needs to be set right.

Adversity, pain, and want are great temptations to transgress one's duty. So it might seem that prosperity, strength, health, and well-being in general, which check the influence of these, could also be considered obligatory ends which make up the duty of promoting *one's own* happiness, and not merely the happiness of others. —But then the end is not the agent's happiness but his morality, and happiness is merely a means for removing obstacles to his morality— a *permissible* means, since no one has a right to demand that I sacrifice my own ends if these are not immoral. To seek prosperity for its own sake is no direct duty, but it can well be an indirect duty: the duty of warding off poverty as a great temptation to vice. But then it is not my happiness but the preservation of my moral integrity that is my end and also my duty.

VI.

ETHICS DOES NOT GIVE LAWS FOR *Actions* (*Ius* DOES THAT), BUT ONLY FOR THE *Maxims* OF ACTIONS

The concept of duty stands in immediate relation to a *law* (even if we abstract from all ends, as its matter) [388]. We have already indicated how, in that case, the formal principle of duty is contained in the categorical imperative: "So act that the maxim of your action could become a universal law." Ethics adds only that this principle is to be conceived as the law of *your own will* and not of will in general, which could also be the will of another. In the latter case the law would prescribe a juridical duty, which lies outside the sphere of ethics. —Maxims are here regarded as subjective principles which merely *qualify* for giving universal law, and the requirement that they so qualify is only a negative principle: not to come into conflict with a law as such. —How then can there be, beyond this principle, a law for the maxims of actions?

Only the concept of an obligatory *end*, a concept that belongs exclusively to ethics, establishes a law for the maxims of actions by subordinating the subjective end (which everyone has) to the objective end (which everyone ought to adopt as his own). The imperative: "You ought to make this or that (*e.g.* the happiness of another) your end" is concerned with the matter of choice (an object). Now no free action is possible unless the agent also intends an end (which is the matter of choice). Hence, when there is an obligatory end, the maxim of the action, in so far as the action is a means to the end, need only qualify for a possible giving of universal law. As opposed to this, it is the obligatory end that can make it a law to have such a maxim, since for the maxim itself the mere possibility

48   [388]

of harmonizing with a giving of universal law is already sufficient.

For the maxims of actions can be *arbitrary*, and come only under the formal principle of action, the limiting condition that they qualify for giving universal law. A *law*, however, does away with this arbitrary element in actions, and by this it is distinguished from *counsels* (which seek to know merely the most appropriate means to an end). [389]

VII.

ETHICAL DUTIES ARE OF *Wide* OBLIGATION, WHEREAS
JURIDICAL DUTIES ARE OF *Narrow* OBLIGATION

This proposition follows from the preceding one; for if the law can prescribe only the maxim of actions, not actions themselves, this indicates that it leaves a play-room (*latitudo*) for free choice in following (observing) the law, *i.e.* that the law cannot specify precisely what and how much one's actions should do toward the obligatory end. — But a wide duty is not to be taken as a permission to make exceptions to the maxim of actions, but only as a permission to limit one maxim of duty by another (*e.g.* love of one's neighbour in general by love of one's parents)—a permission that actually widens the field for the practice of virtue. —As the duty is wider, so man's obligation to action is more imperfect; but the closer to *narrow* duty (Law) he brings the maxim of observing this duty (in his attitude of will), so much the more perfect is his virtuous action.

Imperfect duties, accordingly, are only *duties of virtue*. To fulfill them is *merit* (*meritum* = +a); but to transgress them is not so much *guilt* (*demeritum* = −a) as rather mere *lack* of moral *worth* (=o), unless the agent makes it his principle not to submit to these duties. The strength of one's resolution, in the first case, is properly called only *virtue* (*virtus*); one's weakness, in the second case, is not so much *vice* (*vitium*) as rather mere *want of virtue*, lack of moral strength (*defectus moralis*). (As the word *Tugend* [virtue] comes from *taugen* [to be fit for], so *Untugend* [lack of virtue] comes from *zu nichts taugen* [to be worthless].) Every action contrary to duty is called a *transgression* (*peccatum*). It is when an intentional transgression has been adopted as a basic principle that it is properly called *vice* (*vitium*).

Although the conformity of actions with Law (being a law-abiding man) is not meritorious, the conformity with Law of the maxim of such actions regarded as duties, i.e. <u>reverence</u> for Law, is *meritorious*. For by this we make the right of humanity, or also the rights of men, our *end* and widen our concept of duty beyond the notion of *what is due* (*officium debiti*), since [390] another can demand by right that my actions conform with the law, but not that the law be also the motive for my actions. The same holds true of the universal ethical command: do your duty from the motive of duty. To establish and quicken this attitude in oneself is, again, *meritorious;* for it goes beyond the law of duty for actions and makes the law in itself the motive also.

Hence these duties, too, are of wide obligation. With regard to wide obligation there is present a subjective principle that brings its ethical *reward*—a principle which, to assimilate the concepts of wide and narrow obligation, we might call the principle of receptiveness to this reward in accordance with the law of virtue. The reward in question is a moral pleasure which is more than mere contentment with oneself (this can be merely negative) and which is celebrated in the saying that by this consciousness virtue is its own reward.

If this merit is a man's merit in relation to other men for

promoting their natural and so universally recognized end (for making their happiness his own), it could be called *sweet* merit; for consciousness of it produces a moral gratification in which men are prone to *revel* by sympathetic feeling. But *bitter* merit, which comes from promoting the true welfare of others even when they fail to recognize it as such (when they are unthankful and unappreciative), usually has no such reaction. All that it produces is *contentment* with oneself. But in this case the merit would be still greater.

VIII.

EXPOSITION OF DUTIES OF VIRTUE AS WIDE DUTIES

1. One's Own Perfection as an Obligatory End

a) *Natural* perfection is the *cultivation* of all one's *powers* for promoting the ends that reason puts forward. That natural perfection is a duty and so an end in itself, and that the cultivation of our powers even without regard for the advantage it brings has an unconditioned (moral) imperative rather than a conditioned (pragmatic) one as its basis, [391] can be shown in this way. The power to set an end—any end whatsoever—is the characteristic of humanity (as distinguished from animality). Hence there is also bound up with the end of humanity in our own person the rational will, and so the duty, to make ourselves worthy of humanity by culture in general, by procuring or promoting the *power* to realize all possible ends, so far as this power is to be found in man himself. In other words, man has a duty to cultivate the crude dispositions in human nature by which the animal first raises itself to man. To promote one's natural perfection is, accordingly, a duty in itself.

But this duty is merely ethical or of wide obligation. No

principle of reason prescribes in a determinate way *how far* one should go in cultivating one's powers (in expanding or correcting one's power of understanding, *i.e.* in acquiring knowledge or skill). Then too, the different situations in which men may find themselves make a man's choice of the sort of occupation for which he should cultivate his talents quite arbitrary. With regard to natural perfection, accordingly, reason gives no law for actions but only a law for the maxims of actions, which runs as follows: "Cultivate your powers of mind and body so that they are fit to realize any end you can come upon," for it cannot be said which of these ends could, at some time, become yours.

b) The *cultivation of morality* in us. Man's greatest moral perfection is to do his duty and this *from a motive of duty* (to make the law not merely the rule but also the motive of his actions). —Now at first sight this looks like a *narrow* obligation, and the principle of duty seems to prescribe with the precision and strictness of a law not merely the *legality* but also the *morality* of every action, the attitude of will. But in fact the law, here again, prescribes only the *maxim of the action:* a maxim of seeking the ground of obligation solely in the law and not in sensuous inclination (advantage or prejudice). It does not prescribe the *action itself.* —For man cannot so scrutinize the depths of his own heart as to be quite certain, in even a single action, of the purity of his moral purpose and the sincerity of his attitude, even if he has no doubt about the legality of the action. Very often he mistakes his own weakness, which counsels him against the venture of a misdeed, for virtue (which is the notion of strength); and how many people who have lived long and guiltless lives [392] may not be merely *fortunate* in having escaped so many temptations? It remains hidden from the agent himself how much pure moral content there has been in the motive of each action.

Hence this duty too—the duty of valuing the worth of one's actions not merely by their legality but also by their morality (our attitude of will)—is of only wide obligation. The law does not prescribe this inner action in the human mind itself but only the maxim of the action: the maxim of striving with all one's might to make the thought of duty for its own sake the sufficient motive of every dutiful action.

2. *The Happiness of Others as an Obligatory End*

a) *Natural welfare.* Our *well-wishing* can be unlimited, since in it we need do nothing. But *doing good* to others is harder, especially if we should do it from duty, at the cost of sacrificing and mortifying many of our desires, rather than from inclination (love) toward others. —The proof that beneficence is a duty follows from the fact that our self-love cannot be divorced from our need of being loved by others (*i.e.* of receiving help from them when we are in need), so that we make ourselves an end for others. Now our maxim cannot be obligatory [for others] unless it qualifies as a universal law and so contains the will to make other men our ends too. The happiness of others is, therefore, an end which is also a duty.

[The law says] only that I should sacrifice a part of my well-being to others without hope of requital, because this is a duty; it cannot assign determinate limits to the extent of this sacrifice. These limits will depend, in large part, on what a person's true needs consist of in view of his temperament, and it must be left to each to decide this for himself. For a maxim of promoting another's happiness at the sacrifice of my own happiness, my true needs, would contradict itself were it made a universal law. —Hence this duty is only a *wide* one: since no determinate limits can be assigned to what should be done, the duty has in it a play-room for doing more or less. —The law holds only for maxims, not for determinate actions. [393]

b) The happiness of another also includes his *moral well-being (salubritas moralis)*, and we have a duty, but only a negative one, to promote this. Although the pain a man feels from the pangs of conscience has a moral source, it is still natural in its effect, like grief, fear, or any other morbid state. Now it is not *my* duty to prevent another person from deservedly experiencing this inner reproach: that is *his* affair. But it is my duty to refrain from anything that, considering the nature of men, could tempt him to do something for which his conscience would pain him; in other words, it is my duty not to give scandal. —But this concern for another's moral self-satisfaction does not admit of determinate limits being assigned to it, and so it is the ground of only a wide obligation.

IX.
WHAT IS A DUTY OF VIRTUE?

Virtue is the strength of man's maxims in fulfilling his duty. —We can recognize strength of any kind only by the obstacles it can overcome, and in the case of virtue these obstacles are the natural inclinations, which can come into conflict with man's moral resolution. Now since it is man himself who puts these obstacles in the way of his maxims, virtue cannot be defined merely as self-constraint (for then he could use one natural inclination to restrain another). Virtue is, rather, self-constraint according to a principle of inner freedom, and so by the mere thought of one's duty in accordance with its formal law.

All duties contain a concept of *necessitation* by the law:

ethical duties contain a necessitation such as can take place only in inner legislation—*juridical* duties, a necessitation such that outer legislation is also possible. Both, therefore, contain constraint, whether it be self-constraint or compulsion by another. And since the moral power of self-constraint can be called virtue, action springing from such an attitude (reverence for the law) can be called virtuous (ethical) action, even though the law asserts a juridical duty. For it is the *doctrine of virtue* that commands us to hold man's right holy.

But what it is virtuous to do is not necessarily a *duty of virtue* in the proper sense. The practice of virtue can have to do merely with the *formal* aspect of our maxims, while a duty of virtue is concerned with their matter—that is, with an [394] *end* which is also conceived as a duty. — Now because ethical obligation to ends, of which there can be many, contains merely a law for the maxims of actions and [goes beyond the formal condition of choice] to prescribe an end or matter (object) of choice, it is only *wide* obligation. So, just as there are different ends enjoined by the law, there are many different duties which we call *duties of virtue (officia honestatis)* because they admit of only free self-constraint, not compulsion by others, and because they determine ends which are also duties.

Like anything *formal*, virtue considered as the will's firm resolution to conform with every duty is always *one*. But in relation to the obligatory *end* of action or what one ought to make one's *end* (the material element in the maxim), there can be many virtues. And since obligation to the maxim of such an end is called a duty of virtue, there are many duties of virtue.

The first principle of the doctrine of virtue is: act according to a maxim of *ends* which it can be a universal law for everyone to have. —According to this principle man is an end, to himself as well as to others. And it is not enough that he has no title to use either himself or others merely as means (since according to this he can still be indifferent to them): it is in itself his duty to make man as such his end.

This first principle of the doctrine of virtue, as a categorical imperative, admits of no proof, but it does admit a deduction from pure practical reason. —What, in the relation of man to himself and others, *can be* an end, that *is* an end for pure practical reason. For pure practical reason is a power of ends as such, and for it to be indifferent to ends or to take no interest in them would be a contradiction, because then it would not determine the maxims for actions either (since every maxim contains an end) and so would not be practical reason. But pure reason can prescribe an end *a priori* only in so far as it declares it to be also a duty. And this duty is then called a duty of virtue. [395]

X.

THE FIRST PRINCIPLE OF THE DOCTRINE OF LAW WAS
Analytic: THAT OF THE DOCTRINE OF VIRTUE IS *Synthetic*

We need only the principle of contradiction to see that, if external compulsion checks the hindering of harmonious outer freedom in accordance with universal laws (and is thus an obstacle to the obstacles to freedom), it could harmonize with ends as such. I need not go beyond the concept of freedom to see that anyone may take whatever he pleases as his end. —The first *principle of Law* is therefore an analytic proposition.

But the principle of the doctrine of virtue goes beyond the concept of outer freedom and joins with it, in accordance with universal laws, an *end* which it makes a duty. This principle is therefore synthetic. —Its possibility is contained in the deduction (ix).

It is by laying down obligatory *ends* that pure practical

reason widens the concept of duty beyond the concept of outer freedom and its limitation by the merely formal condition of its thoroughgoing consistency. In place of external compulsion it brings forward *inner* freedom—the power of self-constraint, not through the medium of other inclinations but by pure practical reason (which scorns all these intermediaries). And since Law abstracts altogether from ends, this concept of duty goes beyond juridical duty. —In the moral imperative and the presupposition of freedom necessary on behalf of it, the *law*, the *power* (to fulfill the law), and the *will* determining the maxim comprise all the elements that go to make up the concept of juridical duty. But in that imperative which prescribes *duty of virtue* there is added to the concept of self-constraint the notion of an *end*—not an end that we have but one that we ought to have and that pure practical reason, therefore, has in itself. The highest, unconditioned end of pure practical reason (which is still always duty) consists in this: that virtue should be its own end and also, because of the merit it has among men, its own reward. This end shines so as an ideal that it seems, by human standards, to eclipse *holiness* itself, which is never [396] tempted to transgress the law.* But this is an illusion arising from the fact that, having no way to measure the degree of a strength except by the magnitude of the obstacles it can overcome, we are led to mistake the *subjective* conditions by which we judge a magnitude for the *objective* magnitude itself. Yet in comparison with *human ends*, all of which have their obstacles to be overcome, it is true that the worth of virtue itself, as its own end, far exceeds the value of any utility and any empirical ends and advantages that virtue may, after all, bring about.

---

* Man with all his faults
  Is better than a host of will-less angels. Haller

It is also correct to say that man is under obligation to acquire virtue (as moral strength). For while the *power* (*facultas*) to overcome all opposing sensuous impulses can and must be simply *presupposed* in man on account of his freedom, yet this power as *strength* (*robur*) is something he must acquire. And to acquire it he must exalt the moral *motive* (the thought of the law), both by contemplating the dignity of the pure rational law in him (*contemplatio*) and by *practicing* virtue (*exercitio*). [397]

XI.

According to the principles set forth above, we can diagram the schema of duties of virtue in the following way:

The Material Element of Duty of Virtue

	1	2	
	My own end which is also my duty (My own *perfection*)	*The end of others,* the promotion of which is also my duty (The *happiness* of others)	
Inner Duty of Virtue			Outer Duty of Virtue
	3	4	
	The *law* which is also the motive	The *end* which is also the motive	
	On which the *morality*	On which the *legality*	
	of every free determination of choice is based		

The Formal Element of Duty of Virtue

[398]

XII.

PRELIMINARY CONCEPTS OF THE MIND'S AESTHETIC
RECEPTIVENESS TO CONCEPTS OF DUTY AS SUCH

There are certain moral dispositions such that anyone lacking them could have no duty to acquire them. —They are *moral feeling, conscience, love* of one's neighbour, and *reverence* for oneself (*self-esteem*). There is no obligation to have these because they lie at the basis of morality, as *subjective* conditions of our receptiveness to the concept of duty, not as objective conditions of morality. All of them are natural dispositions of the mind (*praedispositio*) to be affected by concepts of duty—antecedent dispositions on the side of *feeling*. To have them cannot be a duty: every man has them and it is by virtue of them that he can be obligated. —Consciousness of these dispositions is not of empirical origin; rather, it can only follow from consciousness of a moral law, as the effect this has on the mind.

a. Moral Feeling

This is our susceptibility to feel pleasure or pain merely from being aware that our actions are consistent with or contrary to the law of duty. In every determination of choice we go *from* the thought of the possible action to the action by way of feeling pleasure or pain and taking an interest in the action or its effect. Now in this process our *emotional* state (the way in which our inner sense is affected) is either pathological or moral feeling. —*Pathological* feeling precedes the thought of the law: *moral* feeling can only follow from the thought of the law.

Since any consciousness of obligation has moral feeling at its basis, as that which makes us aware of the necessitation present in the concept of duty, there can be no duty to have moral feeling or to acquire it. It is inherent in every man (as a moral being). Our obligation with regard to moral feeling can be only to *cultivate* and strengthen it by our wonder [399] at its inscrutable source. And this wonder arises when we find that moral feeling in its purity, severed from every pathological attraction, is aroused to its full strength by a purely rational thought.

It is not proper to call this feeling moral *sense,* for by the word "sense" we usually mean a theoretical power of perception directed toward an object. But moral feeling (like pleasure and pain in general) is something merely subjective, which yields no knowledge [of objects]. —No man is entirely without moral feeling, for were he completely lacking in capacity for it he would be morally dead. And if (to speak in medical terms) the moral life-force could no longer excite this feeling, then humanity would dissolve (by chemical laws, as it were) into mere animality and be mixed irrevocably with the mass of other natural beings. —But we no more have a special *sense* for the (morally) good and evil than for *truth,* although we often speak in this fashion. We have, rather, a *susceptibility* on the part of free choice to be moved by pure practical reason (and its law), and this is what we call moral feeling.

b. Conscience

In the same way, conscience cannot be acquired and we have no duty to acquire a conscience: every man, as a moral being, has a conscience inherent in him. To be obligated to have a conscience would amount to having the duty of recognizing duties. For conscience is practical reason holding man's duty before him, wherever a law is

applicable, with a view to either his acquittal or his condemnation. Thus it is not directed to an object but merely
to the subject (it affects moral feeling by its act), and so
it is not something incumbent on one, a duty, but rather
an inevitable fact. And when we say: this man has no
conscience, what we mean is: he pays no attention to its
verdict. For if he really had no conscience, then he could
not conceive even the duty of having a conscience, since
he would neither put anything to his credit as in accordance with duty [400] nor reproach himself with anything
as contrary to duty.

I shall here pass over the various divisions of conscience
and note only that the definition of conscience given above
makes an *erring* conscience a logical impossibility. For
while I can indeed err at times in my objective judgment
as to whether something is a duty or not, I cannot err in
my subjective judgment as to whether I have compared
my action with my practical reason (here in its role as
judge) in making the objective judgment. For then I
would have made no practical judgment at all, and in that
case there would be neither truth nor error. *Unconscien-
tiousness* is not a lack of conscience but rather a tendency
to pay no attention to its judgment. But if someone is aware
that he has acted with the approval of his conscience, then
so far as guilt or innocence is concerned nothing more can
be required of him. It is incumbent on him only to en-
lighten his *understanding* in the matter of what is or is not
duty; but when it comes, or has come, to the deed, conscience speaks out involuntarily and inevitably. Therefore,
to act with the approval of one's conscience cannot itself
be a duty; for if it were, there would have to be yet a
second conscience in order for one to become aware of the
act of the first.

Our duty with regard to conscience is only to cultivate it, to sharpen our attentiveness to the voice of the inner judge, and (an indirect duty) to utilize every means to obtain a hearing for it.

c. Love of Man

Love is a matter of *feeling*, not of *will*, and I cannot love because I *will* to, still less because I *ought* to (*i.e.* I cannot be necessitated to love). So a *duty to love* is logically impossible. But *benevolence* (*amor benevolentiae*), as conduct, can be brought under a law of duty. We often call unselfish benevolence to men *love* also (though this is most inappropriate); indeed we speak of love which is also our duty when it is not a question of another's happiness but of the complete and free surrender of all one's ends to the ends of another (even a supernatural) being. But every duty implies *necessitation* or constraint, even if the constraint is to be self-imposed according to a law. And what is done from constraint is not done from love. [401]

To *help* other men according to our ability is a duty, whether we love them or not; and even if it turns out that the human species, on closer acquaintance, does not seem particularly lovable, this would not detract from the force of our duty to help others. —*Hatred of man* is always *hateful*, even if it takes the form merely of a complete withdrawal from men (separatist misanthropy), without active hostility toward them. For benevolence, even toward the misanthropist, remains always a duty; we cannot, indeed, love him, but we can still render good to him.

But to hate vice in men is neither a duty nor contrary to duty; it is rather a mere feeling of aversion from vice, a feeling neither influenced by the will nor exerting influence on the will. *Helping* others to achieve their ends is a

62

duty. If a man practices it often and succeeds in realizing his purpose, he eventually comes to feel love for those he has helped. Hence the saying: you *ought* to *love* your neighbour as yourself, does not mean: you should immediately (first) love him and (afterwards) through the medium of this love do good to him. It means, rather: *do good* to your fellow-man, and this will give rise to love of man in you (as an aptitude of the inclination to beneficence in general). Hence only the love that is mere affection (*amor complacentiae*) is direct. But a duty to this kind of love (which is a pleasure joined immediately with the thought of an object's existence) is a contradiction, since one would have to be necessitated to take pleasure in the object.

d. Reverence

Reverence (*reverentia*), again, is something merely subjective—a special kind of feeling, not a judgment about an object which it would be a duty to produce or promote. For a duty of feeling reverence could be presented to us as a duty only through the *reverence* we feel in the presence of duty. A duty to feel reverence would thus amount to an obligation to [have] duty. —Accordingly it is not correct to say that man has a *duty of self-esteem*. We must rather say that the law in man [402] irresistibly forces from him *reverence* for his own being, and this feeling (of a special kind) is the ground of certain duties, *i.e.* of certain actions in keeping with his duty to himself. We cannot say that man has a duty of reverence for himself, for unless he had in himself reverence for the law he could not even conceive of duty as such.

XIII.

GENERAL PRINCIPLES WHICH A METAPHYSIC OF MORALS MUST FOLLOW IN DEALING WITH A PURE DOCTRINE OF VIRTUE

First. For any one duty there can be *only one* ground of obligation; and if someone produces two or more proofs for the same duty, this is a sure sign either that he has not yet found a valid proof or that he has mistaken two or more different duties for one.

Any moral proof, in so far as it is philosophical, can be adduced only by rational knowledge *from concepts* and not, as in mathematics, by the construction of concepts. Mathematics admits of a number of proofs for one and the same proposition because in *a priori intuition* the structure of an object can be determined in several ways, all of which can be traced back to the same ground. —If, for example, we want to establish the duty of truthfulness first from the *harm* a lie does to others and then also from the *worthlessness* of a liar and his breach of reverence for himself, what we have proved by the first point is a duty of benevolence, not of truthfulness—hence a duty other than the one we wanted to prove. —But it is a highly unphilosophical expedient to resort to a number of proofs for one and the same proposition, consoling oneself that the number of the arguments makes up for the inadequacy of any one of them taken by itself; for this bespeaks cunning and a lack of sincerity. —When several inconclusive arguments are *juxtaposed,* one does not supplement the other's deficiency so as to give certitude or, indeed, even probability. The reasons must *proceed* in *one series,* as *ground* and *consequent,* to a conclusive reason, [403] and

64   [403]

only in this way can they constitute a proof. —Yet the former method is the sleight-of-hand commonly used in the art of persuasion.

Secondly. The distinction of virtue from vice can never be sought in the *degree* to which one follows certain maxims; it must rather be sought only in the specific *quality* of the maxims (their relation to the law). In other words, the celebrated principle (*Aristotle*'s) which locates virtue in the *mean* between two vices is false.* Good management, for example, is said to consist in the *mean* between two vices, prodigality and avarice; as a virtue, then, it cannot be explained as arising either from a gradual diminution of prodigality (from saving) or from an increase of spending on the miser's part—as if these two vices, moving in different directions, met in good management. Rather, each has its own maxim, which necessarily conflicts with the maxims of the others.

For the same reason, no vice as such can be defined in terms of practicing a certain purpose to *excess* (e.g. *prodigalitas est excessus in consumendis opibus*) or of effecting this purpose to a lesser degree than is fitting (e.g. *Avaritia est defectus etc.*). For this definition does not specify the

---

* The formulas commonly used in the language of classical ethics: *medio tutissimus ibis; omne nimium vertitur in vitium; est modus in rebus, etc; medium tenuere beati; insani sapiens nomen ferat, etc.*,[7] contain a superficial wisdom which really has no determinate principles. For who will specify for me this mean between the two outer limits? What distinguishes *avarice* (as a vice) from thrift (as a virtue) is not that avarice carries thrift *too far* but that avarice has an entirely *different principle* (maxim): that of economizing, not for the sake of *enjoying* one's wealth, but merely for the sake of *possessing* it, while denying oneself any enjoyment from it. In the same way, the vice of *prodigality* is not to be sought in an excessive enjoyment of one's wealth but in the bad maxim which makes the use of wealth the sole end, without regard for maintaining the wealth.

degree, while yet it makes the conformity or non-conformity of our conduct with duty depend entirely on its degree. Consequently, this cannot serve as a definition.

Thirdly. We must not determine ethical duties according to our estimate of man's power to fulfill the law; on the contrary, we must estimate man's moral power by the standard of the law, which commands categorically. Hence we must appraise this power on the basis of our rational knowledge of what men should be in keeping with the Idea of humanity, [404] not on the basis of our empirical knowledge of men as they are. These three precepts for a scientific treatment of a doctrine of virtue are contrary to the following ancient dicta:

1) There is only one virtue and one vice.

2) Virtue is the observance of the middle way between opposing vices.

3) Virtue (like prudence) must be learned from experience.

On Virtue as Such[8]

Virtue signifies a moral strength of will. But this does not adequately define the concept, for such strength could also belong to a *holy* (superhuman) being, who would have no hindering impulses to impede the law of his will and who would thus spontaneously do everything according to the law. Virtue is, therefore, the moral strength of a *man's* will in fulfilling his *duty*, a moral *necessitation* by his own legislative reason, in so far as reason constitutes itself a power *executing* the law. To possess this power is not a duty (for then there would have to be an obligation to have duties); rather, reason commands and accompanies its command with a moral constraint (a constraint possible according to laws of inner freedom). But if this constraint

66 [404]

is to be irresistible, as it ought to be, it presupposes strength, in a degree which we can estimate only by the magnitude of the obstacles that man himself creates by his inclinations. The vices, the brood of dispositions contrary to the law, are the monsters which reason has to fight. Accordingly this moral strength, as *courage* (*fortitudo moralis*), is also the greatest and the only true honour that man can win in war, and it is also called true or practical *wisdom*, since it makes the *final end* of man's existence on earth its own end. —Only when man possesses it is he "free," "healthy," "rich," "a king," *etc.;* and only so can he suffer no loss from either chance or fate, since the virtuous man is in possession of himself and his virtue cannot be taken from him.

Our high esteem for the ideal of humanity in its moral perfection can lose nothing of its practical reality by examples to the contrary, drawn from what man now is, has become, or is likely [405] to become in the future; and *anthropology*, which issues from mere experiential knowledge, can do no damage to *anthroponomy*, which is laid down by unconditioned legislative reason. And while virtue (in relation to man, not to the law) can be said here and there to deserve and merit a reward, yet we must consider it in itself; and then, just as it is its own end, it must also be considered its own reward.

Hence virtue in its full perfection is represented, not as if man possesses virtue, but rather as if virtue possesses man; for in the first case it would look as if man still had an alternative (for which he would need yet another virtue in order to choose virtue in preference to all the other wares offered him). —To think of a number of virtues (as we inevitably do) is merely to think of the different moral objects to which the one principle of virtue leads the will,

[405]

and so too with regard to the contrary vices. The personification of virtue and vice is an aesthetic device which, however, does point the way to a moral sense. —Thus an aesthetic of morals, while not indeed a part of the metaphysic of morals, is still a subjective presentation of it in which the feelings that accompany the necessitating power of the moral law (*e.g.* disgust, aversion, *etc.*, which make the moral opposition sensible) make the efficacy of the law felt, in order to win priority away from *merely* sensuous incentives.

XIV.

ON THE PRINCIPLE WHICH DIVIDES THE DOCTRINE OF VIRTUE
FROM THE DOCTRINE OF LAW

This division, on which the over-all division of *moral philosophy* in general also rests, is based on this: that the concept of <u>freedom</u>, which is common to both [the doctrine of Law and the doctrine of virtue], makes it necessary to divide duties into duties of *outer freedom* and duties of *inner freedom*, only the latter of which are ethical. Hence inner freedom, as the condition of all *duties of virtue*, must first be treated in a preliminary note (*discursus praeliminaris*), [406] (just as was done with the doctrine of conscience, as the condition of all duties as such).

Note

On the Doctrine of Virtue *According*
to the Principle of Inner Freedom

An *aptitude* (*habitus*) is a facility in acting and a subjective perfection of the *power of choice*. —But not every such *facility* is a *free* aptitude (*habitus libertatis*); for if it is a *habit* (*assuetudo*),—that is, a uniformity in action which, by the frequent repetition of such actions, tends toward *necessity*—then it is not an aptitude that proceeds from freedom, and so not a moral one. Hence we cannot *define* virtue as an aptitude in free, lawful actions, unless we add "to determine oneself to these actions by the thought of the law." And then this aptitude is not a quality of the power of choice but of the *will*, which is one with the rule it adopts and which is also the appetitive power as it gives universal law. Only such an aptitude can be called virtue.

Inner freedom requires two things of the agent: to be *in control of* himself in any given case (*animus sui compos*)—that is, to *tame* his agitations [*Affekten*]—and to have *mastery* over himself (*imperium in semetipsum*) —that is, to *govern* his obsessions [*Leidenschaften*]. When these two conditions are fulfilled, the *character* (*indoles*) is *noble* (*erecta*); otherwise it is *abject* (*indoles abiecta, serva*).

XV.

VIRTUE REQUIRES, FIRST OF ALL, SELF-MASTERY

Agitations and *obsessions* are essentially different from each other. Agitations belong to *feeling* in so far as it precedes reflection and makes deliberation more difficult or impossible. Hence an agitation is called *precipitate* or *rash* (*animus praeceps*), and reason says, in the [407] concept of virtue, that one *should pull oneself together*. Yet this weakness in the use of one's reason coupled with the strength of one's emotions is only a *lack of virtue* and, as it were, something childish and weak, which can indeed co-exist with the best will. It even has one good thing about it: that this tempest quickly subsides. Accordingly a propensity to an agitation (for example, anger) does not

[407]   69

enter into kinship with vice so readily as does an *obsession*, which is a sensuous appetite that has become a permanent inclination (for example, hatred, as opposed to anger). The calm with which one gives oneself up to it permits reflection and allows the mind to form principles about it and so, if the inclination lights upon something contrary to the law, to brood upon it, to get it rooted deeply, and so to take up the evil (as something premeditated) into its maxim. And the evil is then a *qualified* evil, *i.e.* a true *vice*.

In so far as virtue is based on inner freedom it thus contains a positive command for man, over and above the prohibition against letting himself be ruled by his feelings and inclinations (the duty of *apathy*): the command, namely, to bring all his powers and inclinations under his (that is, reason's) control—hence the command of self-mastery. For unless reason holds the reins of government in its own hands, man's feelings and inclinations assume mastery over him.

XVI.

VIRTUE NECESSARILY PRESUPPOSES APATHY
(REGARDED AS STRENGTH)

The word "apathy" has fallen into disrepute, as if it meant lack of feeling and so subjective indifference regarding objects of choice: it has been taken for weakness. We can prevent this misunderstanding by giving the name *"moral apathy"* to that freedom from agitation which is to be distinguished from indifference, for in it the feelings arising from sensuous impressions lose their influence on moral feeling only because reverence for the law prevails over all such feelings. The strength of feeling that raises a lively interest in the *good* itself to an agitation [408]—or, better, allows this interest to degenerate into an agitation

70   [408]

—is only the illusory strength of one sick with a fever. This kind of agitation is called *enthusiasm;* and the *moderation* that is often commended as if it were the practice of virtue itself should be taken in this context (*insani sapiens nomen ferat aequus iniqui—ultra quam satis est virtutem si petat ipsam. Horat.*) For otherwise it is absurd to suppose that one could be *too wise, too virtuous.* Agitation always belongs to sensibility, no matter by what kind of object it is aroused. The true strength of virtue is a *tranquil mind* with a deliberate and firm resolution to put the law of virtue into practice. That is the state of *health* in the moral life, while an agitation, even one aroused by the thought of the *good,* is a momentary and glittering phenomenon that leaves lassitude behind it. —But that man can be called fantastically virtuous who admits *nothing* morally *indifferent* (*adiaphora*) and strews all his steps with duties, as with man-traps; it is not indifferent, to him, whether I eat meat or fish, drink beer or wine, supposing that both agree with me. Fantastic virtue is a micrology which, were it admitted into the doctrine of virtue, would turn the sovereignty of virtue into a tyranny.

Note

Virtue is always in *progress* and yet always beginning *from the beginning.*—It is always in progress because, considered *objectively,* it is an ideal which is unattainable, while yet our duty is constantly to approximate to it. That it is always beginning anew has a *subjective* basis in human nature, which is affected by inclinations under whose influence virtue can never settle down in peace and quiet, with its maxims adopted once and for all— unless it is climbing, it inevitably sinks. For moral maxims, unlike technical ones, cannot be based on habit (since habit belongs to the natural quality of the will's determination): on the contrary, if the practice of virtue were to become habit the agent would suffer loss to the *freedom* in adopting maxims which characterizes an action done from duty. [409]

XVII.
CONCEPTS PRELIMINARY TO THE DIVISION
OF THE DOCTRINE OF VIRTUE

The *first* thing the principle of division must do concerns what is *formal* [in the doctrine of virtue]: it must contain all the conditions which serve to distinguish this part of moral philosophy in general from the doctrine of Law, and do so according to the specific form of this part. It does this by laying it down: 1) that duties of virtue are duties for which there is no outer legislation; 2) that the law which all duties must yet have as their basis can, in ethics, be a law of duty given merely for the maxims of actions and not for actions; 3) that (as follows in turn from this) ethical duty must be conceived as *wide*, not as narrow, duty.

The *second* thing concerns what is *material* [in the doctrine of virtue]. The principle must present the doctrine of virtue not merely as the doctrine of duty in general but also as the *doctrine of ends*, and show that man is obligated to regard himself, as well as every other man, as his end. These obligatory ends are usually called duties of self-love and of love for one's neighbour; but this is not using the terms in their strict sense, since there can be no direct duty to love. Our direct duty is, rather, to actions by which we make ourselves and others our end.

The *third* thing concerns the *division* of the material from the formal (purposefulness from lawfulness)[9] in the

72   [409]

principle of duty. Regarding this, it should be noted that not every *obligation of virtue (obligatio ethica)* is a duty of virtue *(officium ethicum s. virtutis)*: reverence for law as such does not yet establish an end as a duty, and only an obligatory end is a duty of virtue. —Hence there is only *one* obligation of virtue, whereas there are *many* duties of virtue; for there are indeed many objects which it is our duty to have as our ends, but only *one* virtuous attitude of will, as the subjective ground determining us to fulfill our duty. This ethical obligation extends over juridical duties too, but it does not entitle them to be called duties of virtue. —Hence all the *divisions* of ethics will concern only duties of virtue. The science of the way in which obligation is imposed without regard for possible external legislation is ethics itself, viewed according to its formal principle. [410]

Note

But, it will be asked, why do I divide Ethics into the *Doctrine of Elements* and the *Doctrine of Method*, when no such division was needed in the Doctrine of Law? — The reason is that the doctrine of Law deals with *narrow* duties only, whereas ethics has to do with *wide* duties. Hence the doctrine of Law, which by its nature must determine duties strictly (precisely), has no more need of general precepts (methodology) as to how we should proceed in judgment than has pure mathematics; it realizes these precepts in action. But ethics, because of the *play-room* it allows in its imperfect duties, inevitably leads judgment to pose the question of how a maxim should be applied in particular cases; and since the answer gives us another (subordinate) maxim, we can always inquire again after a principle for applying this maxim to cases that may come up. And so ethics falls into *casuistry*, which has no place in the doctrine of Law.

Thus *casuistry* is neither a *science* nor a part of a science; for in that case it would be dogmatics, and it is not so much a doctrine of how *to discover* something as rather *practice* in the proper way of *seeking* truth. Hence it is *woven into* ethics only in a *fragmentary* way, not systematically (as a part of ethics proper would have to be), and is added to ethics only as scholia to the system.

But the *Doctrine of Method* of morally-practical reason deals not so much with judgment as rather with reason and its exercise in both the *theory* and the *practice* of its duties, and so it belongs properly to ethics. The *first* exercise of reason comprises what can be called the *erotematic* method and consists in drawing forth from the pupil, by questioning, what he already knows about concepts of duty.[10] If he knows it because he has previously been told it, so that now it is drawn merely from his memory, the method is the *catechetical* method proper; if it is presupposed that the knowledge is already contained naturally in the pupil's reason and needs only to be developed from it, the method is called that of *dialogue* (the Socratic method).

Didactic[11], as an exercise in theory, has *ascetic* for its practical counterpart. This part of the Doctrine of [411] Method teaches not merely the concept of virtue but also how to put into practice and cultivate the *capacity for* and the *will to* virtue.

In accordance with these principles we shall present the system in two parts: the *Ethical Doctrine of Elements* and the *Ethical Doctrine of Method*. Each part will be divided into its sections, and these in turn will be divided into various chapters. In the first part, the division of chapters will be based on the different *subjects* to whom man is obligated: in the second part, on the different *ends* which reason constrains man to have and his receptivity to these ends.

XVIII.

Now the division that practical reason traces out to establish an ethical system of its concepts (the architectonic division) can be made according to two different principles, taken either singly or together. One sets forth the *subjective* relation of the obligating agent to the obligated agent according to the *matter* of the system; the other sets forth the *objective* relation of the ethical law to duty as such according to the *form* of a system. —The *first* division is that of the *beings* in relation to which an ethical obligation is conceivable; the *second* would be the division of the *concepts* of pure ethically-practical reason which concern these ethical duties. These concepts are, accordingly, required in ethics only in so far as it should be a *science*, and so are required for the methodic arrangement of all the propositions found on the basis of the first division. [412]

First Division of Ethics According to the Distinction of the Subjects and the Corresponding Laws

It contains duties

of man to men   of man to beings other than men

to himself   to other   sub-human beings   super-human beings
        men

Second Division of Ethics According to Principles of a System of Pure Practical Reason
Ethical

Doctrine of Elements	Doctrine of Method
Dogmatics Casuistry	Didactic[12] Ascetic

Because the latter division concerns the form of the science, it must precede the former, as the ground-plan of the whole.

I

THE ETHICAL DOCTRINE
OF ELEMENTS

PART I

On Duties to Oneself as Such

INTRODUCTION

§ 1.

The Concept of a Duty to Oneself Might Seem (at First Glance) to Contain a Contradiction

If the *obligating* I is taken in the same sense as the *obligated* I, the concept of duty to oneself contains a contradiction. For the concept of duty contains the notion of being passively necessitated (I am *obligated*). But if the duty is a duty to myself, I conceive myself as *obligating* and so as actively necessitating (I, the same subject, am imposing the obligation). And the proposition that asserts a duty to myself (I *ought* to obligate myself) would contain an obligation to be obligated (a passive obligation that would yet, in the same sense of the relation, also be an active obligation), and hence a contradiction. —We can also bring this contradiction to light by pointing out that the obligating subject (*auctor obligationis*) could always release the obligated subject (*subiectum obligationis*) from the duty (*terminus obligationis*), so that if both are one and the same subject, one would not really be obligated to a duty he imposes on himself. And this contains a contradiction.

§ 2.
Nevertheless, Man Has Duties to Himself

For supposing there were no such duties: then there would be no duties whatsoever, and so no external duties either. —For I can recognize that I am under obligation to others only in so far as I, at the same time, obligate myself, since the law by virtue of which I deem myself obligated always [417] proceeds from my own practical reason; and in being necessitated by my own pure practical reason, I am also the necessitating subject in relation to myself.*

§ 3.
Solution to This Apparent Antinomy

When man is conscious of a duty to himself, he views himself, as the subject of duty, under two aspects: first as a *sensuous being [Sinnenwesen]*, *i.e.* as man (a member of one of the animal species), and secondly as a *purely rational being [Vernunftwesen]* (not merely as a being endowed with reason, since reason in its theoretical function might well be the quality of a living corporeal being). The senses cannot attain this latter aspect of man: it reveals itself only in morally-practical relations, where the incomprehensible property of *freedom* makes itself known by the influence of reason on the will legislating within him.

Now man as a *natural being* endowed with reason (*homo phaenomenon*) can be determined by the *causality* of his

---

* Thus when it is a question, for example, of vindicating my honour or of preserving myself, I say: "I owe it to myself." Even in what concerns duties of less importance, those that are only meritorious and not essential, I speak the same way: for example, "I owe it to myself to increase my aptitude for social intercourse and so forth (to cultivate myself)."

[417]

reason to actions in the sensible world, and so far the notion of obligation does not come into consideration. But the same man considered in terms of his *personality*, *i.e.* as a being endowed with *inner freedom* (*homo noumenon*), is susceptible of obligation and, indeed, of obligation to himself (to humanity in his own person). Thus man (taken in these two different senses) can consistently recognize a duty to himself (because he does not conceive "man" in one and the same way).

§ *4.*
Of the Principle on Which the Division of Duties to Oneself is Based

The division can be made only with respect to objects of duty, not with regard to the self-obligating subject. The [418] obligated, as well as the obligating, subject is always *only* man; and though we are allowed, in theoretical knowledge, to distinguish soul and body from each other, as natural characteristics of man, we are not allowed to think of them as distinct substances imposing obligation on him, so as to justify a division of duties to the *body* and duties to the *soul*. Neither experience nor rational inference gives us adequate grounds for deciding whether man has a soul (in the sense of a substance dwelling in him, distinct from the body and capable of thinking independently of it, *i.e.* a spiritual substance), or whether it is not much rather the case that life may be a property of matter. And even if the first alternative be true, it is still inconceivable that man should have a duty to a *body* (as an obligating subject), even to a human body.

1) There will, accordingly, be only one *objective* division of duties to oneself—a division into what is formal and what is <u>material</u> in duties to oneself. The first of these

are *limiting* (negative duties); the second, *widening* (positive duties to oneself). The negative duties *forbid* man to act contrary to the end of his nature and so have to do merely with his moral *self-preservation;* the positive duties, which *command* him to make a certain object of choice his end, concern his *perfecting* of himself. Both of them pertain to virtue—the first as duties of omission (*sustine et abstine*), the second as duties of commission (*viribus concessis utere*); both, however, are duties of virtue. The first pertain to the moral health (*ad esse*) of man as the object of both his outer and inner sense, to the *preservation* of his nature in its perfection (as *receptivity*). The second belong to his moral *wealth* (*ad melius esse, opulentia moralis*), which consists in having the *power* to realize all his ends, in so far as this can be acquired; they belong to his *cultivation* of himself (as active perfecting). The principle of negative duties to oneself lies in the dictum: live according to nature (*naturae convenienter vive*), *i.e. preserve* yourself in the perfection of your nature; that of positive duties to oneself, in the saying: *make yourself more perfect* than mere nature made you (*perfice te ut finem, perfice te ut medium*).

2) But there will be a *subjective* division of man's duties [419] to himself, *i.e.* one in terms of whether the subject of duty (man) views himself as an animal (natural) and at the same time moral being, or merely as a moral being.

Now there are impulses of nature having to do with man's animality. These are instincts by which nature aims at: a) the preservation of the subject, b) the preservation of the species, and c) the preservation of the subject's ability to enjoy the pleasures of life, though still on the animal level only.[13] —The vices that here conflict with

82

man's duty to himself are *self-murder*, the unnatural use of his *sexual desire*, and such *immoderate consumption of food and drink* as weakens his capacity for using his powers purposefully.

But man's duty to himself *merely* as a moral being (in abstraction from his animality) consists in what is *formal* in the harmony of the maxims of his will with the *dignity* of humanity in his person. It is, therefore, a prohibition against robbing himself of a moral being's *prerogative*—that of acting in accordance with principles (*i.e.* inner freedom)—and so making himself a plaything of the mere inclinations and hence a thing. The vices contrary to this duty are lying, avarice, and false humility (servility). Since these vices are directly contrary to man's character as a moral being (according to its very form)—that is, contrary to inner freedom, the inherent dignity of man—to take them as one's principles amounts to making it one's principle to have no principle and so no character. It is to throw oneself away and make oneself an object of contempt. —The virtue that is opposed to all these vices could be called *love of honour* (*honestas interna, iustum sui aestimium*), an attitude far removed from *ambition* (*ambitio*) (which can be quite abject). But we shall discuss this at greater length later on, under the appropriate heading. [420]

BOOK I
ON PERFECT DUTIES TO ONESELF

§ 5.

The *first*, though not the highest, of man's duties to himself as an animal being is *to preserve himself* in his animal nature.

The opposite of this is arbitrary *physical death* or self-destruction (*autochiria*), which can be either total or partial. —Total self-destruction is *suicide* (*suicidium*). Partial self-destruction is *mutilating* oneself; and this, in turn, can be either *material*, depriving oneself of certain integral, organic *parts* (*i.e.* maiming oneself), or *formal*, depriving oneself (permanently or temporarily) of one's *capacity* for the natural *use* (and so indirectly for the moral *use*) of one's powers.

Since in this chapter we are speaking only of negative duties and so of duties of omission, the discussions of duties must be directed against the vices opposed to duty to oneself. [421]

Article I. On Suicide
§ 6.

Arbitrary *suicide* can be called <u>self-murder</u> (*homocidum dolosum*) only if we can show that it is generally a wrong committed either upon one's own person or also, by the destruction of one's own person, upon others (as when a pregnant woman kills herself).

a) Suicide is a wrong (murder). It can, indeed, also be treated as a violation of one's duty to other men (the duty of a married couple to each other, of parents to their

84   [421]

children, of subjects to their ruler or fellow-citizens, and finally as a violation of duty to God, if we think of man as leaving the post assigned him in the world without having been called away from it). But since we are here speaking only of a transgression of duty to oneself, the question is whether, prescinding from all those considerations, man is still obligated merely by his quality as a person to preserve his life and whether he must recognize in this a duty (and indeed a strict duty) to himself.

It seems absurd to say that a man could wrong himself (*volenti non fit iniuria*). Hence the Stoic thought it a prerogative of his own personality (the Sage's) to depart as he pleased from life (as from a smoke-filled room) with peace of soul, free from the pressure of present or anticipated ills, simply because he could be of no more use in life. —But in this very courage and strength of soul, by which he scorned death and knew of something that man can value still higher than his life, he must have found a still stronger reason not to destroy a being with so much power and authority over the strongest sensuous motives, and so not to deprive himself of life.

Man cannot renounce his personality so long as he is a subject of duty, hence so long as he lives; and that he should have the moral title to withdraw from all obligation, *i.e.* freely to act as if he needed no moral title for this action, is a contradiction. [422] To destroy the subject of morality in one's own person is to root out the existence of morality itself from the world, so far as this is in one's power; and yet morality is an end in itself. Consequently, to dispose of oneself as a mere means to an arbitrary end is to abase humanity in one's own person (*homo noumenon*), which was yet entrusted to man (*homo phaenomenon*) for its preservation.

It is a form of partial self-murder to deprive oneself of

an integral, organic part (or mutilate oneself), for example, to give away or sell a tooth to be transplanted into another person's mouth or to be castrated in order to make a more comfortable living as a singer and so forth. But to have a dead or diseased organ amputated when it endangers one's life or to have something cut off which is a part, but not an organ, of the body (*e.g.* one's hair) cannot be considered a wrong against one's own person—although a woman who cuts her hair in order to sell it is not altogether free from guilt.

Casuistical Questions

Is it self-murder to hurl oneself to certain death (like Curtius) in order to save one's country?—or is voluntary martyrdom, offering oneself as a sacrifice for the welfare of the whole human race, also to be considered an act of heroism?

Is it permissible to anticipate by suicide the unjust death sentence of one's ruler—even if the ruler permits this (as did Nero with Seneca)?

Can a great, recently dead king[14] be charged with a wrong intention for having kept a strong poison at hand, presumably so that if he were captured when he led his troops into battle he could not be forced to agree to conditions of ransom prejudicial to his country?—for can one ascribe this purpose to him without having to presume mere pride behind it?

A man who had been bitten by a mad dog already felt hydrophobia, and he explained, in a letter he left, that since, so far as he knew, the disease was incurable, he killed himself [423] lest he harm others as well in his madness, the onset of which he already felt. Did he do wrong?

Anyone who decides to be vaccinated against smallpox

86   [423]

puts his life in danger, even though he does it *to preserve his life;* and, in so far as he himself brings on the disease that endangers his life, he is in a far more doubtful situation, so far as the law of duty is concerned, than is the sailor, who at least does not arouse the storm to which he entrusts himself. Is smallpox inoculation, then, permissible?

Article II. On Carnal Self-Defilement

§ 7.

Just as the natural function of the love of life is to preserve the *individual,* so the natural function of sexual love is to preserve the *species:* in other words, both of these are *natural purposes.* By a natural purpose I mean such a connection of the cause with an effect that, without attributing intelligence to the cause, we must yet conceive it by analogy with an intelligent cause and so as if it produced the effect purposefully. The question now is whether the agent's use of his sexual power comes under a limiting law of duty with respect to his own person, or whether he can, without violating a duty to himself, use his sexual power for mere animal pleasure, without regard for its purpose. —The doctrine of Law establishes that a man cannot use *another* person for this pleasure, apart from a special limitation by a legal contract in which the two reciprocally obligate each other. But here we are asking whether, with regard to this gratification, man has a duty to himself, the violation of which is a *defilement* (not merely an abasement) of humanity in his own person. The instinct to this pleasure is called *carnal lust* (or also simply lust). The vice generated through it is called *impurity;* the virtue with regard to this sensuous impulse is called *chastity,* which is now to be set forth as a duty of man to himself. Lust is called *unnatural* if man is aroused to it, not by its real

[424] object, but by his imagination of this object, and so in a way contrary to the purpose of the desire, since he himself creates its object. For in this way the imagination brings forth an appetite contrary to nature's purpose, and indeed an appetite that is still more important than love of life itself, since it aims at the preservation of the whole species and not only of the individual.

That such an unnatural use (and so misuse) of one's sexual power is a violation of duty *to oneself* and, indeed, one which is contrary to morality in the highest degree occurs to everyone immediately, along with the thought of it, and stirs up an aversion from this thought to such an extent that we consider it indecent even to call this vice by its proper name. This does not happen in the case of self-murder, which we do not hesitate in the least to lay before the world's eyes in all its heinousness (as a *species facti*[15]). In the case of unnatural vice it is as if man in general felt ashamed of being able to treat his own person in such a way, which degrades it beneath the beasts. Thus when it is necessary to speak, in a well-bred society, of even the permissible (but in itself, admittedly, merely animal) physical union of the two sexes in marriage, this occasions and calls for great delicacy, in order to throw a veil over it.

But it is not so easy to produce the rational proof that the unnatural, and even the merely purposeless, use of one's sexual power is a violation of duty to oneself (and indeed, so far as the first is concerned, a violation in the highest degree). —The *ground of proof*, of course, is that man surrenders his personality (throwing it away) by using himself merely as a means to satisfy his animal instincts. But this does not explain the high degree of the violation of humanity in one's own person involved in unnatural vice, which by its form (the attitude embodied in it) seems to surpass even self-murder in its viciousness. It consists, then, in this: that the man who defiantly casts off the burden of life is at least not making a feeble surrender to animal impulse in throwing himself away; self-murder requires courage, and in this attitude there is always room for reverence for humanity in one's own person. But unnatural vice, which is complete abandonment of oneself to animal inclination, makes man not only an object of enjoyment but, still further, an unnatural thing, *i.e.* a *loathsome* object, and so deprives him of all reverence for himself. [425]

Casuistical Questions

Nature's purpose in the intercourse of the sexes is procreation, *i.e.* the preservation of the race. Hence one may not, at least, act contrary to that end. But is it permissible to use the sexual power *without regard for that end* (even within marriage)?

For example, if the wife is pregnant or sterile (because of age or sickness), or if she feels no desire for intercourse, is not the use of the sexual power contrary to nature's purpose and so also contrary to duty to oneself as well, in one way or another—just as in unnatural lust? Or is there, in this case, a permissive law of morally-practical reason, which in the clash of its determining grounds makes permissible something that is in itself not permitted (indulgently, as it were), in order to prevent a still greater transgression? At what point can we call the limitation of a wide duty a *purism* (a pedantry in the observance of duty, so far as the wideness of the duty is concerned) and allow the animal inclinations a play-room, at the risk of abandoning the law of reason?

Sexual inclination is also called "*love*" (in the narrowest sense of the term) and is, in fact, the strongest possible senuous pleasure in an object. It is not merely a *pleasure of the senses*, such as we experience in objects that are pleasing when we merely contemplate them (capacity for which pleasure is called taste). It is rather pleasure from the *use* of another person, which therefore belongs to the *appetitive* power and, indeed, to the appetitive power in its highest degree, passion. But it cannot be classed with either the love that is mere affection or the love of benevolence (for both of these stop short of carnal enjoyment). It is a unique kind of pleasure (*sui generis*), and the passion really has nothing in common with moral love, though it can enter into close union with it under the limiting conditions of practical reason. [426]

Article III. On Self-Stupefaction by the Immoderate Use of Food and Drink

§ 8.

Our reason for considering this kind of intemperance a vice is not the harm or bodily pain (diseases of this kind) that man brings on himself by it; for in that case the principle for counteracting intemperance would be one of well-being and comfort (and so of happiness), and such a principle can be the ground only of a rule of prudence, never of a duty—at least not of a direct duty.

Brutish intemperance in the use of food and drink is the misuse of the means of nourishment, whereby our ability to use them rationally is hindered or exhausted. *Drunkenness* and *gluttony* are the vices that come under this heading. Man in a drunken condition is to be treated as a mere animal, not as a man; as a result of overindulgence in food he is, for a certain time, incapacitated for such actions as would require adroitness (skill) and deliberation in the use of his powers. —That it is a violation of duty to oneself to put oneself in such a condition leaps to the eye. The first of these degradations below even animal nature is commonly brought about by fermented drinks, but it can also result from other narcotics, such as opium and other vegetable products. The temptation to use these lies in the fact that they produce, for a time, a state of fancied happiness, a freedom from care, and even an illusory strength; but dejection and weakness follow and, worst of all, a need to repeat the narcotics and in so doing to increase them is established. Gluttony is even lower than drunkenness in so far as it engages merely sense as a passive condition and not, as does drunkenness, the imagination, which does afford an *active* play of representations; hence gluttony is even closer to the pleasure of cattle. [427]

Casuistical Questions

Can we at least justify, if not extol, a use of wine bordering on intoxication, on the ground that it enlivens the company's conversation and combines it with frankness? —Or can we even grant it the merit of promoting what Horace praises in Cato: *virtus eius incaluit mero?*[16] —But who can determine the *measure* for a man who is only too ready to pass into a state where he has no clear eye for *measuring?*[17] The use of opium and spirits comes closer to degradation since the illusory state of well-being they produce makes the user silent, reticent, and withdrawn: they are therefore permissible only as medicines. —Mohammedanism, which forbids wine altogether, thus made a bad choice in allowing opium to take its place.

Although a banquet is a formal invitation to intemperance in both food and drink, there is still something in it that aims at a moral end, beyond mere physical well-being:

it keeps a lot of people together for a long time so that they may exchange their ideas. And yet the very number of the guests (if, as Chesterfield says, it exceeds the number of the muses[18]) permits only a limited exchange of ideas (between people sitting next to each other); and so the arrangement is at variance with that [moral] end, while the banquet remains a temptation to immorality—intemperance, which is a violation of duty to oneself. How far can we extend the moral title to accept these invitations to intemperance?

CHAPTER II

ON MAN'S DUTY TO HIMSELF CONSIDERED MERELY
AS A MORAL BEING

This duty is opposed to the vices of *lying, avarice*, and *false humility* (servility).[428]

1. On Lying

§ *9.*

The greatest violation of man's duty to himself merely as a moral being (to humanity in his own person) is the contrary of truthfulness, the *lie* (*aliud lingua promptum, aliud pectora inclusum gerere*[19]). In the doctrine of Law an intentional untruth is called a lie only if it infringes on another's right. But it is clear of itself that in ethics, which derives no moral title to an action from its harmlessness [to others], every deliberate untruth in the expression of one's thoughts deserves this harsh name. For dishonour (being an object of moral scorn), which accompanies it, also accompanies the liar like his shadow. —The lie can be an outer lie (*mendacium externum*) or also an inner lie. By a lie a man makes himself contemptible—by an outer lie, in the eyes of others; by an inner lie, in his own eyes, which is still worse—and violates the dignity of humanity in his own person. And so, since the harm that can come to others from it is not the characteristic property of this vice (for if it were, the vice would consist only in violating one's duty to others), we do not take this harm into account here. Neither do we consider the harm that the liar brings on himself; for then a lie, as a mere error in prudence, would be contrary to the pragmatic maxim, not to the moral maxim, and it could not be considered a violation of duty at all. —By a lie a man throws away and, as it were, annihilates his dignity as a man. A man who himself does not believe what he tells another (even a merely ideal Person) has even less worth than if he were a mere thing. For a thing, as something real and given, has the property of being serviceable and another person can make some use of it. But the man who communicates his thoughts to someone in words which yet (intentionally) contain the contrary of what he thinks on the subject has a purpose directly opposed to the natural purposiveness of the power of communicating one's thoughts and therefore renounces his personality and makes himself a mere deceptive appearance of man, not man himself. —*Truthfulness* in expressing one's thoughts is also called *"honesty"* and, if this expression of thought is also a promise, *trustworthiness;* but, more generally, truthfulness is called *sincerity*. [429]

A lie (in the ethical sense of the term), an intentional untruth as such, need not be *harmful* to others in order to be pronounced reprehensible; for then it would be a violation of the rights of others. A lie may arise from mere frivolity or even good nature; indeed, the speaker may intend to achieve a really good end by it. But his way of pursuing the end is, by its mere form, a wrong to his own person and a baseness which must make him contemptible in his own eyes.

It is easy to show that man is, in fact, guilty of many

inner lies, but to explain the possibility of an inner lie seems more difficult. For a lie requires a second person whom one intends to deceive, and intentionally to deceive oneself seems to contain a contradiction.

Man as a moral being (*homo noumenon*) cannot use his natural being (*homo phaenomenon*) as a mere means (a speaking machine), as if it were not bound to its intrinsic end (the communication of thought): he is bound to use his natural being in a way that is consistent with the pronouncement (*declaratio*) of his moral being and obligated to himself to *truthfulness*. If, for example, a man who really does not believe in a future judge of the world professes a lying belief in such a judge, persuading himself that it could do no harm and might indeed be useful to profess such a belief in the presence of a scrutinizer of hearts, in order hypocritically to win His favour if He should happen to exist, [this man is guilty of an inner lie. And the same is true] if, being in no real doubt about the existence of this future judge, he flatters himself that he inwardly reverences His law, though the only motive he feels is fear of punishment.

Insincerity is a mere lack of *conscientiousness, i.e.* of sincerity in our avowals before our *inner* judge, whom we conceive as another person when we think of sincerity in its utmost strictness. Strictly speaking, it is already insincerity if, for example, from self-love we take a wish for the deed because this wish has a good end in mind. In this case the inner lie—although it is really contrary to man's duty to himself—gets the name of a frailty, as when a lover's wish to find only good qualities in his beloved blinds him to her obvious faults. —But this insincerity in his avowals, which man perpetrates upon himself, still deserves the most serious blame, since it is from such a foul spot (falsity, which seems to be rooted in human [430] nature itself) that the evil of deceitfulness spreads into man's relations with other men, when once the principle of truthfulness has been violated.

Note

It is noteworthy that the Bible dates the first crime, by which evil entered the world, not from *fratricide* (Cain's) but from the first *lie* (for nature still rebels against fratricide), and calls the author of all evil a liar from the beginning and the father of lies. Reason can assign no further ground for man's propensity to *hypocrisy* (*esprit fourbe*), although this propensity must have been present first; for an act of freedom cannot (like a natural effect) be derived and explained according to the natural law of the connection of effects with their causes, all of which are appearances.

Casuistical Questions

Can an untruth from mere politeness (*e.g.* the "your obedient servant" at the end of a letter) be considered a lie? No one is really deceived by it. —An author asks one of his readers; "How do you like my work?" One could merely pretend to give an answer, by joking about the impropriety of such a question. But who has his wit always ready? The author will be insulted at the slightest hesitation with one's answer. May one, then, say what the author would like to hear?

If I tell a lie in more serious matters, which concern the Mine and Thine, must I answer for all the consequences it might have? For example, a householder has ordered his servant to say "not at home" if a certain man asks for him. The servant does this and, as a result, the caller slips

away and commits a serious crime, which would otherwise have been prevented by the guard sent to arrest him.
On whom (according to ethical principles) does the blame
fall in this case? On the servant, surely, who violated a
duty to himself by his lie, the results of which his own
conscience imputes to him. [431]

II. On Avarice
§ 10.

By avarice in this context I do not mean *greedy avarice*
(acquiring the means of good living in excess of one's true
needs), for this can also be viewed as a mere violation of
one's duty (of beneficence) *to others;* nor, again, do I
mean *miserly avarice*, which is called *stinginess* or niggardliness when it is shameful but which can still be mere
neglect of one's duties of love to others. I mean, rather, the
restricting of *one's own* use of the means to good living
so narrowly as to leave one's true needs unsatisfied. It is
really this kind of avarice, which is contrary to duty *to
oneself*, that I am referring to here.[20]

The censure of this vice illustrates clearly that virtue,
as well as vice, can never be defined in terms of mere
<u>degree</u>, and at the same time it proves the uselessness of
the *Aristotelian* principle that virtue consists in the middle
way between two vices.

For if I regard *good management* as the mean between
prodigality and avarice and suppose this mean to be one
of *degree*, then one vice would pass over into the (*contrarie*) opposite vice only through the *virtue;* and so virtue
would be simply a diminished, or rather a growing, vice.
The result, in the present case, would be that the real duty
of virtue would consist in making no use whatsoever of
the means of good living.

If we want to distinguish vice from virtue, the difference we must recognize and explain is not a difference in the *degree* of practicing moral maxims but rather in the objective *principle* of the maxims. —The *maxim of greedy avarice* (prodigality) is to get and keep all the means to good living *with the purpose of enjoying them.*[21] —The maxim of miserly avarice, on the other hand, is to get and keep all the means to good living, but *without regard to this enjoyment* (*i.e.* in such a way that one's end is only to possess the means, not to use them).

Hence the characteristic mark of miserly avarice is the principle of possessing the means to all sorts of ends, but with the reservation [432] that one wills not to use them and so to deprive oneself of the comforts necessary to enjoy life; and this is directly contrary to duty to oneself with regard to the end.* Thus prodigality and miserliness are not distinguished from each other by their degree; they are rather distinguished specifically, by their opposing maxims.

---

* The proposition: one ought not to do too much or too little of anything says, in effect, nothing, for it is a tautology. What does it mean "to do too much"? Answer: to do more than is good. What does it mean "to do too little"? Answer: to do less than is good. What does it mean to say "I *ought* (to do or to refrain from something)"? Answer: "that it is not good (that it is contrary to duty) to do more or less than is good." If that is the wisdom in search of which we should go back to the ancients (Aristotle), as to those who were nearer the fountainhead: *virtus consistit in medio, medium tenuere beati, est modus in rebus, sunt certi denique fines, quos ultra citraque nequit consistere rectum,* then we have made a bad choice in turning to its oracle. —Between truthfulness and lying (as *contradictorie oppositis*) there is no mean; but there is indeed a mean between candour and reticence (as *contrarie oppositis*), since one who declares his thoughts can say only what is true without telling the *whole truth.* Now it is quite natural to ask the teacher of ethics to point out this mean to me. But this he cannot do; for both duties of virtue have a play-room in their application (*latitudo*), and what is to be done cannot be de-

Casuistical Questions

Self-seeking (*solipsismus*) is the ground both of the greed (insatiability in acquiring wealth) which has sumptuous living as its end and of niggardliness (painful anxiety about waste); [433] and both of them—prodigality as well as miserliness—may seem to be reprehensible merely because they end in poverty, though in the case of prodigality this result is unexpected and in the case of miserliness it is deliberately chosen (the agent wills to live like a pauper). And so, since we are here speaking only of duty to oneself, it may be asked whether either prodigality or miserliness should be called vice at all, or whether both are not rather mere imprudence and so quite beyond the bounds of duty to oneself. But miserliness is not merely mistaken thrift: it is a slavish subjection of oneself to riches, which is a violation of duty to oneself since one ought to be master of them. It is opposed to *liberality* of mind (*liberalitas moralis*) as such (not to generosity, *liberalitas sumtuosa*, which is only an application of this to a

---

termined according to rules of morality (moral rules); only judgment can decide this according to rules of prudence (pragmatic rules). In other words, what is to be done cannot be decided after the manner of narrow duty (*officium strictum*), but only in the way of *wide* duty (*officium latum*). Hence one who follows the principles of virtue can, it is true, make a *mistake* (*peccatum*) in putting these principles into practice, by doing more or less than prudence prescribes. But in so far as he adheres strictly to these principles he cannot commit a *vicious* act (*vitium*), and Horace's verse: *insani sapiens nomen ferat aequus iniqui, ultra quam satis est virtutem si petat ipsam,* is basically false, if taken literally. In fact, *sapiens* here means only a *judicious* man (*prudens*), who does not think fantastically of virtue in its perfection. This is an ideal which requires us to approximate to this end but not to attain it completely, since the latter requirement surpasses man's powers and introduces a lack of sense (fantasy) into the principle of virtue. For really to be *too virtuous*—that is, to be too faithful to one's duty—would be equivalent to making a circle too round or a straight line too straight.

particular case); it is opposed, in other words, to the principle of independence from everything except the law, and is a fraud that the subject perpetrates on himself. But what kind of a law is it that the inner legislator itself does not know how to apply? Ought I to economize on food or only in my expenditures on external things? in old age, or already in youth? Or is thrift as such a virtue?

III. On Servility

§ *11.*

Man in the system of nature (*homo phaenomenon, animal rationale*) is a being of slight importance and shares with the rest of the animals, as offspring of the earth, a common value (*pretium vulgare*). Although man has, in his reason, something more than they and can set his own ends, even this gives him only an *extrinsic* value in terms of his usefulness (*pretium usus*). This extrinsic value is the value of one man above another—that is, his *price* as a ware that can be exchanged for these other animals, as things. But, so considered, man still has a lower value than the universal medium of exchange, money, the value of which can therefore be called preeminent (*pretium eminens*).

But man regarded as a *person*—that is, as the subject of morally practical reason—is exalted above any price; for as such (*homo noumenon*) he is not to be valued as a mere means to the ends of others [434] or even to his own ends, but as an end in himself. He possesses, in other words, a *dignity* (an absolute inner worth) by which he exacts *respect* for himself from all other rational beings in the world: he can measure himself with every other being of this kind and value himself on a footing of equality with them.

[434]

Humanity in his own person is the object of respect, and he can demand this respect from every other man; but he must, also, do nothing by which he would forfeit this respect. Hence he can and should value himself by a low as well as by a high standard, depending on whether he views himself as a being of the sensible world (in terms of his animal nature) or as an intelligible being (in terms of his moral disposition).—When, as he must do, he regards himself not merely as a person as such but also as a man—that is, as a person who has duties laid upon him by his own reason—his insignificance as a *natural man* cannot detract from his consciousness of his dignity as a *moral man*, and he should not disavow his moral self-esteem regarding the latter: he should seek his end, which is in itself a duty, not abjectly, not in a *servile spirit* (*animo servili*) as if he were seeking a favour, not disavowing his dignity, but always with consciousness of his sublime moral disposition (which is already contained in the concept of virtue). And this *self-esteem* is a duty of man to himself.

The consciousness and feeling of one's insignificant moral worth in *comparison* with the <u>law</u> is *humility* (*humilitas moralis*). To be convinced of the greatness of one's moral worth, but only for want of comparing it with the law, can be called *moral arrogance* (*arrogantia moralis*). — The disavowal of all claim to any moral worth in oneself, in the belief that one will thus acquire a borrowed worth, is morally *false humility* (*humilitas spuria*).

<u>Humility</u> in *comparing oneself with other men* (and indeed with any finite being, even a seraph) is no duty; rather, the man who tries to equal or surpass others in humility, believing that in this way he will also acquire a greater inner worth, is guilty of *pride* (*ambitio*), which

100

is directly contrary to his duty to others. But deliberately to set aside one's own moral worth merely as a means to acquiring the favour of another, [435] no matter who he may be (hypocrisy and flattery [*Heuchelei* and *Schmei-chelei*]*) is false (lying) humility, which is contrary to duty to oneself since it is an abasement of one's personality.

True humility follows inevitably from our sincere and strict comparison of ourselves with the moral law (its holiness and strictness). But along with it comes exaltation and the highest self-esteem, as the feeling of our inner worth (*valor*), when we realize that we are capable of this inner legislation, and the (natural) man feels himself compelled to reverence the (moral) man in his own person. By virtue of this worth we are not for sale at any price (*pretium*) and possess an inalienable dignity (*dignitas interna*) which instills in us reverence (*reverentia*) for ourselves.

§ *12.*

This duty to ourselves regarding the dignity of humanity within us can be recognized, more or less, in the following examples.

Be no man's lackey. —Do not let others tread with impunity on your right. —Contract no debt for which you cannot give full security. —Do not accept favours you could do without, and do not be a parasite or a flatterer or (what really differs from these only in degree) a beggar. Be thrifty, then, so that you will not become destitute. —

---

* "*Heucheln*," properly "*häuchlen*" ["to dissemble"] seems to be derived from "*Hauch*," a moaning "breath" interrupting one's speech (a pious ejaculation). '*Schmeicheln*" ["to flatter"] stems from "*Schmiegen*" ["to bend"] which, as a habit, is called "*Schmiegeln*" ["cringing"] and finally, in High German, "*Schmeicheln*."

Complaining and whining—even a mere cry in bodily pain—is unworthy of you, especially if you know you have deserved the pain; thus a criminal's death may be ennobled (its disgrace averted) by the resoluteness with which he dies. —Kneeling down or prostrating oneself on the ground, even as an outward sign of veneration for holy things, is contrary to the dignity of humanity, as is invoking these in the presence of images; for you then humble yourself, not before an *Ideal* presented [436] by your own reason, but before an *idol* of your own making.

Casuistical Questions

May not man's feeling for his sublime destiny, *i.e.* his *elation of spirit* (*elatio animi*) or esteem for himself, come so close to *self-conceit* (*arrogantia*)—the very opposite of true *humility* (*humilitas moralis*)—that it is inadvisable to cultivate self-esteem even when we compare ourselves with other men, and not only when we compare ourselves with the law? Or is it not more likely that this kind of self-abnegation, confirming others' opinion of us, would encourage them to despise our person and so constitute a violation of our duty (of reverence) to ourselves? In any case, bowing and scraping before a man seems beneath man's dignity.

Preferential tributes of respect in words and manners even to those who have no authority in the State—reverences, obeisances (compliments) and courtly phrases marking with the utmost precision every distinction in status (something altogether different from courtesy, which must also be reciprocal)—the *Du, Er, Ihr* and *Sie*, or *Ew. Wohledeln, Hochedeln, Hochedelgeborenen, Wohlgeborenen* (*ohe, iam satis est!*) as forms of address, a pedantry in which the Germans seem to outdo any other people

[436]

in the world (except possibly the Indian castes): does not all this prove that there is a widespread propensity to servility in men? (*Hae nugae in seria ducunt.*²²)But one who makes himself a worm cannot complain if people step on him.

CHAPTER II

SECTION I. ON MAN'S DUTY TO HIMSELF

AS HIS OWN INNATE JUDGE

§ *13.*

Every concept of duty contains objective necessitation by the law (as a moral imperative limiting our freedom) and belongs [437] to practical reason, which gives the rule. But the inner *imputation* of a deed, as a case that comes under the law (*in meritum aut demeritum*), belongs to the *power of judgment* (*iudicium*), which, as the subjective principle imputing an action, judges with legal effect whether an action considered as a deed (an action coming under a law) took place or not. On this there follows the verdict of *reason* (the sentence), which (as condemnation or acquittal) joins with the action its legal effect. All of this takes place before a *tribunal* (*coram iudicio*), which, as a moral person giving effect to the law, is called a *court of justice* (*forum*). —Consciousness of an *inner court* in man ("before which his thoughts accuse or excuse one another") is <u>conscience</u>.

Every man has a conscience and finds himself watched, threatened, and, in general, kept in an attitude of respect (of esteem coupled with fear) by an inner judge; and this power watching over the law in him is not something that he himself (arbitrarily) *makes*, but something incorporated in his being. It follows him like his shadow when he plans to escape. He can indeed numb himself or put himself to sleep by pleasures and distractions, but he cannot avoid coming to himself or waking up from time to time; and when he does, he hears at once its fearful voice. He can at most, in the extremity of corruption, induce himself to pay no more attention to it, but he still cannot help *hearing* it.

Now this inherent intellectual and (since it is the thought of duty) moral disposition called *conscience* has something peculiar about it: although its business is an affair of man with himself, man yet sees himself necessitated by his reason to carry it on as if at the bidding of *another person*. For this action is the bringing of a *case* (*causa*) before a court; and to think of the man *accused by* his conscience as *one and the same person* with the judge is an absurd way of representing a court of justice, since then the prosecutor would always lose.—Hence for every duty man's conscience will have to conceive someone *other* than himself (*i.e.* other than man as such) as the judge of his actions; otherwise it would be in contradiction with itself. This other may be a [438] real person or a merely ideal person which reason itself produces.*

---

* The man who accuses and judges himself in conscience must think of himself as a twofold personage, a doubled self who, on the one hand, has to stand in fear and trembling at the bar of the tribunal which is yet entrusted to him, but who, on the other hand, must himself administer the office of judge which he holds by inborn authority. And this requires clarification, if reason is not to fall into self-contradiction. —I, the prosecutor and yet the accused as well, am the same *man* (*numero idem*). But man as the subject of the moral legislation which proceeds from the concept of freedom and in which he is subject to a law that he himself gives (*homo noumenon*) is to be considered different (*specie diversus*) from man as a member the sensible world who is endowed with reason. But it is only from the viewpoint of practical knowledge that he is to be regarded in this way, since there is no theoretical knowledge of the causal relation of the intelligible to the sensible; and this specific difference is that of the human faculties (the higher and the lower) which characterize man. The first is the prose-

Such an ideal person (the authorized judge of conscience) must be a scrutinizer of hearts, since the court of
justice is set up *within* man. But at the same time he must
impose all obligation: since conscience is the inner judge
of all free actions, he must be, or must be conceived as, a
person in relation to whom all our duties are to be regarded as also his commands. —Now since such a moral
being must also have all power (in heaven and on earth)
in order to be able to give his law its due effect (a function
essential to the office of judge), and since such an omnipo-
tent moral being is called <u>God</u>, conscience must be conceived as a subjective principle of responsibility before
God for our deeds. In fact the latter concept will always be
contained (even if only in an obscure way) in the moral
self-awareness of conscience.

This is not to say that man is entitled, on the grounds
of the Idea to which his conscience inevitably leads him, to
posit such a Supreme Being as *really existing* outside himself—still less that he is *obligated* to do so. For the Idea is
not given to him *objectively*, by theoretical reason, but
only *subjectively*, by practical reason which obligates
[439] itself to act in conformity with this Idea. And only
by way of analogy with a lawgiver for all rational beings
in the world does this Idea merely guide man to think of
conscientiousness (which is also called *religio*) as responsibility before a holy Being (morally legislative reason)
distinct from man yet present in his inmost being, and to
submit himself to the will of this Being, as the rules of

---

cutor, against whom the accused is granted a legal adviser (defence
counsel). When the proceedings are concluded the inner judge, as
the person vested with authority, pronounces the sentence of happiness or misery, as the moral consequences of the deed. Our reason cannot pursue further his authority (as ruler of the world) in this function;
we can only reverence his unconditioned *iubeo* or *veto*.

justice. Man's conception of religion as such is here only "a principle of regarding all his duties *as if* they were divine commands."

1) In a case involving conscience (*causa conscientiam tangens*) we think of conscience as *warning* us (*praemonens*) before our decision. And in cases where conscience is the sole judge (*casibus conscientiae*), the utmost *scrupulosity* (*scrupulositas*) where the concept of duty (something moral in itself) is concerned cannot be considered hair-splitting (a micrology), nor can a real transgression be considered a bagatelle (*peccatilium*) and be left to a conscience that offers only arbitrary counsels (according to the principle *minima non curat praetor*). Hence ascribing a *wide* conscience to someone amounts to calling him *unconscientious*.

2) When the deed is completed the *prosecutor* first comes forward in conscience, but along with him comes the *defence counsel* (advocate); and their dispute cannot be settled amicably (*per amicabilem compositionem*), but must rather be decided according to the rigor of the Law. And on this there follows

3) the legally effective verdict of conscience on the man—his *acquittal* or *condemnation*—which concludes the case. With regard to this verdict it should be noted that an acquittal can never assign him a *reward* (*praemium*), something gained that he did not have before. It brings only a *rejoicing* at having escaped the danger of being found deserving of punishment. Hence the bliss found in the comfort and encouragement of conscience is not *positive* (joy) but merely *negative* (relief from preceding anxiety); and only virtue, as a struggle against the influence of the evil principle in man, can confer this. [440]

SECTION II. ON THE FIRST COMMAND OF
ALL DUTIES TO ONESELF

§ *14.*

This command is: *know* (scrutinize, fathom) *yourself,* not in terms of your natural perfection (your fitness or unfitness for realizing all your arbitrary and obligatory ends), but rather in terms of your moral perfection, in relation to your duty. Know your heart—whether it is good or evil, whether the source of your actions is pure or impure. Know what can be imputed to you and what belongs to your moral state, whether as something inherent in man's *substance* or as something derived (acquired or admitted [into his being]).

Moral self-knowledge, which requires one to penetrate into the unfathomable depths and abyss of one's heart, is the beginning of all human wisdom. For wisdom consists in the harmony of the will of a being with his final end, and in the case of man this requires him first to remove the inner obstacle (an evil will actually present in him) and then to develop his inalienable and inherent disposition of a good will. "Only the descent into the hell of self-knowledge can pave the way to deification."

§ *15.*

This moral self-knowledge will, first, dispel *fanatical* contempt for oneself as a man (for the whole human race); for such contempt is self-contradictory. —Only man's splendid disposition for the good, which makes him worthy of respect, can lead him to find a man who acts contrary to this contemptible (the man himself, but not humanity in him). —But, secondly, this knowledge will also counteract the self-esteem, arising from *self-love,* that consists in taking mere wishes—wishes which, however ardent, always remain ineffectual—for proof of a good heart. (*Prayer*, too, is only a wish declared inwardly before a scrutinizer of hearts.) Impartiality in judging oneself in comparison with the law and sincerity in avowing to oneself one's inner moral worth or unworth are [441] duties to oneself that follow immediately from that first command of self-knowledge.

EPISODIC SECTION

ON THE *Amphiboly* OF THE MORAL *Concepts of Reflection*,
WHICH CONSISTS IN REGARDING CERTAIN OF OUR DUTIES TO
MEN AS DUTIES TO BEINGS OTHER THAN MEN

§ *16.*

So far as mere reason can judge, man has duties only to men (himself and other men); for his duty to any subject is moral necessitation by that subject's will. Hence the necessitating (obligating) subject must, *first*, be a person; and this person must, *secondly*, be given as an object of experience, since man is supposed to further the end of that person's will, and this can happen only in the relation of two existing beings (for a merely conceptual being cannot *cause* any effect in the order of ends). But with all our experience we know of no being other than man that would be susceptible of obligation (active or passive). Therefore man can have no duty to beings other than men. If he thinks he has such duties, it is because of an *amphiboly of the concepts of reflection*, and his alleged duty to other beings is really a duty to himself. He is led to this misunderstanding by mistaking his duty *with regard to* other beings for duty *to* those beings.

Now this alleged duty can be referred to objects *other than persons* or to objects which are indeed persons, but quite *imperceptible* ones (that cannot be presented to the outer senses). —The first (*sub-human*) objects can be mere inorganic matter (minerals), or matter organized for reproduction though still without sensation (plants), or the part of nature endowed with sensation and choice (animals). The second (*super-human*) objects can be conceived as spiritual beings (angels, God). —We must now ask whether man has a relation of duty with these two kinds of beings, and with which of them. [442]

§ *17.*

A propensity to wanton destruction of the *beautiful* in inanimate nature (*spiritus destructionis*) is opposed to man's duty to himself; for it weakens or destroys man's disposition to love things (*e.g.* beautiful crystal formations, the indescribable beauty of plants) without regard for their utility. And while this feeling is not in itself moral, it is still a disposition of sensibility that greatly promotes or at least prepares the way for morality.

With regard to the animate but irrational part of creation, violent and cruel treatment of animals is far more intimately opposed to man's duty to himself, since it dulls his sympathetic participation in their pain and so weakens and gradually destroys a natural disposition most useful to morality in one's relations with other men. It is within man's moral title to kill animals quickly (without pain) and to put them to work that does not strain them beyond their powers (such work as man himself must do). But painful physical experiments for the sake of mere speculation, when the end can be achieved as well without these, are to be abhorred. —Even gratitude for the long service of an old horse or dog (just as if they were members of the household) belongs *indirectly* to man's duty *with regard to* these animals. Considered as a *direct* duty, however, it is always only a duty of man *to* himself.

§ *18.*

Again, we have a duty *with regard to* what lies entirely beyond the limits of our experience but is yet encountered, according to its possibility, in our Ideas, *e.g.* the Idea of God. It is called the duty of religion: the duty "of recognizing all our duties *as if* (*instar*) they were divine commands." But this is not consciousness of a duty *to God*. For this Idea proceeds entirely from our own reason and *we ourselves make it,* whether for the theoretical purpose of explaining to ourselves the purposiveness in the universe as a whole or also for the [practical] purpose of serving as the motive in our conduct. [443] Hence we do not have before us, in this Idea, a given being <u>to</u> whom we would be under obligation; for in that case the reality of this being would first have to be shown (revealed) by experience. Rather, it is a duty of man to himself to apply this Idea, which reason inevitably holds out to him, to the moral law in him, where it is of the greatest moral fruitfulness. In this (<u>practical</u>) sense it can therefore be said: to have religion is a duty of man to himself.

BOOK II
ON MAN'S IMPERFECT DUTIES TO HIM-SELF (WITH REGARD TO HIS END)
SECTION I.

ON MAN'S DUTY TO HIMSELF TO DEVELOP AND INCREASE HIS *Natural Perfection*—THAT IS, HIS DUTY TO HIMSELF FROM A PRAGMATIC POINT OF VIEW

§ *19.*

Man has a duty to himself of cultivating (*cultura*) his natural powers (powers of mind, soul, and body), which are the means to all sorts of possible ends. —Man owes it to himself (as a rational being) not to leave idle and, as it were, rusting away the natural dispositions and powers that his reason can in any way use. Even supposing that the native scope of his powers is sufficient for his natural needs, his reason must first show him, by principles, that this meager scope of his powers is *sufficient;* for, as a being who is able to set ends (to make objects into his ends), he is indebted for the use of his powers not merely to natural instinct but rather to the freedom by which he determines this scope. Hence the ground on which man should develop his powers is not regard for the *advantage* [444] that can be gained by cultivating them; for (according to Rousseau's principles) the advantage might turn out on the side of his crude natural needs. Rather, it is a command of morally practical reason and a *duty* of man to himself to cultivate his powers (among them, one more than the other, in so far as men have different ends) and to be, from a pragmatic point of view, a man equal to the end of his existence.

The *powers of the mind* are those whose exercise is possible only through reason. They are creative to the extent that their use is not drawn from experience but rather derived *a priori* from principles, of the sort that comprise mathematics, logic, and the metaphysics of nature. The latter two are also counted as philosophy, namely theoretical philosophy. In this case "philosophy" does not mean wisdom, as the word itself would suggest, but only science. However, theoretical philosophy can help to promote the ends of wisdom.

The *powers of the soul* are those which are at the disposal of the understanding and the rule it uses to fulfill its chosen purposes, and to this extent they have experience as their guide. To the powers of the soul belong memory, imagination and the like, on which we can build learning, taste (inner and outer embellishment) and so forth, which are tools for manifold purposes.

Finally, cultivating the *powers of the body* (gymnastic in the proper sense) is looking after the basic *stuff* (the matter) in man, without which he could not realize his ends. Hence man has a duty to himself constantly and purposefully to maintain his animal vigour.

§ 20.

As to which of these natural perfections should take *precedence* among our ends and in what *proportion* to one another we should make them our ends in keeping with our duty to ourselves, it remains for us to choose, according to our rational deliberation about what sort of life we should like to lead and whether we have the powers necessary for that way of life (*e.g.* whether it should be manual labour, commerce, or scholarship). For, quite apart from the need to support himself, which in itself cannot be the ground of a duty, [445] man has a duty to himself to be a useful member of the world, since this also belongs to the worth of humanity in his own person, which he ought not to degrade.

But man's duty to himself regarding his *natural* perfection is only a *wide* and imperfect duty. For while it does contain a law for the maxims of actions, it determines nothing about the kind and extent of the actions themselves but leaves a play-room for free choice.

SECTION II.

ON MAN'S DUTY TO HIMSELF TO INCREASE HIS *Moral*
PERFECTION—THAT IS, HIS DUTY TO HIMSELF
MERELY FROM A MORAL POINT OF VIEW

§ 21.

In the *first* place, this duty consists, *subjectively*, in the
purity (*puritas moralis*) of one's attitude in duty: that even
without any admixture of purposes derived from the sensuous inclinations, the law is of itself the motive and actions
are done not merely in conformity with duty but also
from the motive of duty. —Here the command is "be
holy." *Secondly* this duty is concerned, *objectively*, with
the whole moral end of perfection—that is, with perform-
ing all one's duties and achieving the complete moral end
in relation to oneself. Here the command is "be perfect."
But man's striving after this end always remains only a
progress from *one* perfection to others. "If there be any
virtue, and if there be any praise, think on these things."

§ 22.

This duty to oneself is a *narrow* and perfect one in its
quality; but it is wide and imperfect in its degree, and this
because of the *frailty* (*fragilitas*) of human nature.

It is man's duty to *strive for* this perfection, but not to
achieve it (in this life), and his pursuit of perfection,
accordingly, is only a continual progress. Hence while this
duty is indeed a narrow and perfect one *with regard to*
the object (the Idea which one should make it one's end to
realize), *in relation to* the subject it is only a wide and imperfect duty to oneself.

The depths of the human heart are [446] unfathomable.
Who knows himself well enough to say whether his

motive for fulfilling his duty proceeds entirely from the thought of the law or whether there are not many other impulses, of sensuous origin, co-operating with it—motives that look to advantage (or to avoiding disadvantage) and that, in other circumstances, could just as well serve vice? —As for what concerns perfection as a moral end, it is true that in the Idea (objectively) there is only *one* virtue (as the moral strength of one's maxims); but in reality (subjectively) there are a number of virtues of different characters. And among these virtues it might always be possible to find at least one moral weakness, if we wanted to look for it (though, because of those virtues, such weaknesses are not commonly called vice).[23] But if our self-knowledge is never adequate to show us whether we possess the sum-total of virtues, the sum-total of virtues can be the ground only of an imperfect duty to be perfect.

All duties to oneself regarding the end of humanity in one's own person are, therefore, only imperfect duties. [447]

PART II
On Duties of Virtue to Others

CHAPTER I
ON DUTIES TO OTHERS MERELY AS MEN
SECTION I. ON DUTIES OF LOVE TO OTHER MEN
Division
§ *23.*

The first division of duties of virtue to others can be the division into duties by fulfilling which we also obligate the other, and duties whose observance does not result in obligation on the other's part. —To fulfill the first is *meritorious* (in relation to the other person); but to fulfill the second is to render the other only what is *due* to him. —*Love* and *respect* are the feelings that accompany the practice of these duties. They can be considered separately (each by itself) and can also exist separately (we can *love* our neighbour though he might deserve but little respect, and we can show him the *respect* necessary for every man though we might not think him very lovable). But in their ground in the law love and respect are always joined together in a duty, only in such a way that now one duty and now the other is the subject's principle, with the other joined to it as an accessory. —Thus we shall recognize an obligation to help a poor man; but since our favour humbles him by making his welfare dependent on our generosity, it is our duty to behave as if our help is either what is [448] merely due to him or but a slight service of love, and so to spare him humiliation and maintain his self-respect.

§ 24.

When we are speaking of laws of duty (not laws of nature) and, among these, of laws governing men's external relations with one another, we are considering a moral (intelligible) world where, by analogy with the physical world, *attraction* and *repulsion* bind together rational beings (on earth). The principle of <u>mutual love</u> admonishes men constantly to *come nearer* to each other; that of the <u>respect</u> which they owe each other, to keep themselves at a *distance* from one another. And should one of these great moral forces fail, "then nothingness (immorality), with gaping throat, would drink the whole kingdom of (moral) beings like a drop of water" (if I may use Haller's words, but in a different connection[24]).

§ 25.

In this context, however, <u>love</u> is not to be taken as a *feeling* (aesthetic love), *i.e.* a pleasure in the perfection of other men; it does not mean *emotional* love (for others cannot oblige us to have feelings). It must rather be taken as a maxim of *benevolence* (practical love), which has beneficence as its consequence.

The same holds true of the <u>respect</u> to be shown to others: it is not to be taken merely as the *feeling* that comes from comparing one's own *worth* with another's (such as mere habit causes a child to feel toward his parents, a pupil toward his teacher, a subordinate in general toward his superior). Respect is rather to be taken in a practical sense

[448]

(*observantia aliis praestanda*), as a *maxim* of limiting our self-esteem by the dignity of humanity in another person.

Moreover, the duty of free respect to others is really only a negative one (of not exalting oneself above others) and is thus analogous to the juridical duty of not encroaching on another's possessions. Hence, although respect is a [449] mere duty of virtue, it is considered *narrow* in comparison with a duty of love, and it is the duty of love that is considered *wide*.

The duty of love for one's neighbour can also be expressed as the duty of making others' *ends* my own (in so far as these ends are only not immoral). The duty of respect for my neighbour is contained in the maxim of not abasing any other man to a mere means to my end (not demanding that the other degrade himself in order to slave for my end).

By the fact that I fulfill a duty of love to someone I obligate the other as well: I make him indebted to me. But in fulfilling a duty of respect I obligate only myself, contain myself within certain limits in order to detract nothing from the worth that the other, as a man, is entitled to posit in himself.

On Duties of Love in Particular
§ 26.

Since we are now conceiving love of man (philanthropy) as practical, not emotional, love, we must locate it in active benevolence so that it has to do with the maxims of actions. —A man who finds satisfaction in the well-being (*salus*) of men simply as men and is glad when things go well for them is called a *friend of man* (philanthropist) in general. A man who is pleased only when things go ill with others is called an *enemy of man* (a misanthropist in the practical sense). A man who is indifferent to the welfare of others if only things go well for himself is a *self-seeker* (*solipsista*). —But a man who avoids other men because he can find no *pleasure* in them, though he indeed *wishes* them *well*, would be a *cynic* (an aesthetic misanthropist), and his aversion from men could be called anthropophobia.

§ 27.

According to the ethical law of perfection "love your neighbour as yourself," every man has a duty to others of adopting the maxim of benevolence (practical love of man), whether or not he finds them lovable. —For every morally-practical [450] relation to men is a relation of men in the thought of pure reason, *i.e.* a relation of free actions according to maxims which qualify for giving universal law and which, therefore, cannot be self-seeking (*ex solipsismo prodeuntes*). I want every other man to be benevolent to me (*benevolentiam*); hence I should also be benevolent to every other man. But since all *other* men with the exception of myself would not be *all* men, and the maxim would then not have the universality of a law, as it must have in order to be obligatory, the law prescribing the duty of benevolence will include myself, as the object of benevolence, in the command of practical reason. —Not that I am thereby obligated to love myself (for this happens inevitably, apart from any command, and so there is no obligation to it); it is rather that legislative reason, which includes the whole species (and so myself with it) in its Idea of humanity as such (not of men), includes me, when it gives universal law, in the duty of mutual benevolence, according to the principle that I am equal with all others besides me, and *permits* you to be benevolent to *yourself* under the condition of your being benevolent to every other man as well. For it is only in this way that your maxim (of benevolence) qualifies for giving universal law—the principle on which every law of duty is based.

§ 28.

Now the benevolence present in the love of all men as such is indeed the greatest in its *extent,* but the smallest in its *degree;* and when I say: I take an interest in this man's welfare only in keeping with my universal love for man, the interest I take in him is as slight as an interest can be. I am only not indifferent with regard to him.

Yet one man is closer to me than another, and in benevolence I am the closest to myself. Now how does this fit in with the precept "love your *neighbour* (your fellowman) as yourself"? When (in the duty of benevolence) one man is closer to me than another, I am obligated to greater benevolence to him than to the other; but I am admittedly closer to myself (even according to duty) than any other. So it would seem that I cannot, without contradicting myself, say that I ought to love every man as myself; for the standard of self-love would allow of no difference in degree. —But it is quite obvious [451] that what is meant, in this case, is not a mere benevolence in *wishes,* which is really only a satisfaction in the well-being of all others and does not even require me to contribute to their well-being (every man for himself: God for us all). It refers, rather, to active, practical benevolence (beneficence), which consists in making another's well-being and happiness my *end*. For in wishing I can be *equally* benevolent to everyone, whereas in acting I can, without violating the universality of my maxim, vary the degree greatly according to the different objects of my love (one of whom concerns me more closely than the other).

Division of Duties of Love

They are duties of a) *beneficence,* b) *gratitude,* and c) *sympathy.*

A. On the Duty of Beneficence
§ 29.

To provide oneself with such comforts as are necessary merely to enjoy life (to take care of one's body, but not to the point of effeminacy) is a duty to oneself. The contrary of this is to deprive oneself of the essential pleasures of life, whether from avarice (of the slavish kind) or from exaggerated (fanatical) discipline of one's natural inclinations. Both of these are opposed to man's duty to himself.

But how can it be required, as a duty, that we go beyond *benevolence* in our wishes regarding others (which costs us nothing) and make this benevolence practical, so that everyone who has the means should be *beneficent* to the needy? —Benevolence is satisfaction in another's happiness (well-being); but beneficence is the maxim of making another's happiness one's end, and the duty of beneficence is the necessitation that reason exercises on the agent to adopt this maxim as universal law.

It is not self-evident that any such law is to be found in reason; on the contrary, the maxim "Every man for himself: God (fortune) for us all" seems to be the most natural one. [452]

§ 30.

It is every man's duty to be beneficent—that is, to promote, according to his means, the happiness of others who are in need, and this without hope of gaining anything by it.

120

For every man who finds himself in need wishes to be helped by other men. But if he lets his maxim of not willing to help others in turn when they are in need become public, *i.e.* makes this a universal permissive law, then everyone would likewise deny him assistance when he needs it, or at least would be entitled to. Hence the maxim of self-interest contradicts itself when it is made universal law—that is, it is contrary to duty. Consequently the maxim of common interest—of beneficence toward the needy—is a universal duty of men, and indeed for this reason: that men are to be considered fellow-men—that is, rational beings with needs, united by nature in one dwelling place for the purpose of helping one another.

§ 31.

The *rich* man (the man supplied abundantly with means for the happiness of others—that is, beyond his own needs) should hardly ever regard his beneficence as meritorious duty, even though in practicing it he does put others under obligation. The satisfaction he derives from his beneficence, which costs him no sacrifice, is a kind of revelling in moral feelings. —He must also carefully avoid any appearance of intending to put the other under obligation, for if he showed such an intention (thereby humbling the other in his own eyes) he would not be extending true beneficence. Rather, he must make it felt that he is himself obliged by the other's acceptance or honoured by it, hence that the duty is merely something that he owes. But it is still better if he can practice his beneficence in complete secrecy. —This virtue is greater when the benefactor's means are limited and he is strong enough quietly to take on himself the hardship he spares the other. Then he can really be considered morally *rich*. [453]

Casuistical Questions

How far should we expend our means in practicing beneficence? Surely not to the extent that we ourselves would finally come to need the charity of others. How much worth has beneficence extended with a cold hand (by a will to be put into effect at one's death)? —What of the man who deprives another of his *freedom* but, in exercising over him the supreme authority permitted by the law of the land, does so according to his own idea of how to make that person happy (of how to do good to his bondsman)? Can this man consider himself beneficent for taking paternal care of his bondsman in keeping with *his own* concept of happiness? Or is not the injustice of depriving someone of his freedom a thing so opposed to juridical duty as such that the man who freely consents to submit to this condition, counting on his master's beneficence, commits the supreme rejection of his own humanity, and the master's utmost concern for this man would not really be beneficence at all? Or could the service which the master renders him be so great as to outweigh man's right? —I cannot do good to anyone according to *my* concept of happiness (except to young children and the insane), but only according to that of the one I intend to benefit; and I am not really being kind to someone if I force a gift on him.

The ability to practice beneficence, which depends on property, follows largely from the injustice of the government, which favours certain men and so introduces an inequality of wealth that makes others need help. This being the case, does the rich man's help to the needy, on which he so readily prides himself as something meritorious, really deserve to be called beneficence at all?

B. On the Duty of Gratitude

Gratitude consists in *honoring* a person because of a kindness he has done us. The feeling connected with this recognition is respect for the benefactor (who puts one under obligation). But the benefactor is viewed as only in a relation of [454] love to the one who receives his favour. —Even a mere heartfelt *benevolence* on another's part, without material results, deserves to be called a duty of virtue; and this is the basis for the distinction between *active* gratitude and the gratitude of mere *affection*.

§ 32.

Gratitude is a duty. It is not a mere *prudential* maxim of encouraging another to show me further beneficence by attesting my indebtedness to him for a past kindness (*gratiarum actio est ad plus dandum invitatio*); for in such a maxim I use him merely as a means to my further purposes. Gratitude is, rather, immediate necessitation by the moral law, *i.e.* duty.

But gratitude must also be considered, more especially, a *holy* duty—that is, a duty such that its transgression (as a scandalous example) can destroy in principle the moral motive to beneficence. A moral object is holy if the obligation with regard to it cannot be discharged completely by any act in conformity with the obligation (so that no matter what he does, the person who is under obligation always remains under obligation). Any other duty is an *ordinary* duty. —But one cannot, by any requital of a kindness received, rid oneself of the obligation for this kindness, since one can never win away from the benefactor his *priority* of merit: the merit of having been the first in benevolence. —Even a mere heartfelt benevolence, apart from any such

[454]   123

act (of beneficence), is already a ground of obligation to gratitude. A grateful attitude of this kind is called *appreciativeness*.

§ 33.

So far as the *extension* of this gratitude is concerned, it reaches not merely to our contemporaries but also to our ancestors, even to those we cannot identify with certainty. It is for this reason, too, that we think it improper not to defend the ancients, whom we can regard as our teachers, from all attacks, accusations, and disdain, in so far as this is possible. But it is foolish to attribute a pre-eminence in talents and good will to the ancients in preference to the moderns—as if the world were steadily declining, [455] according to laws of nature, from its original perfection— and to despise everything new in comparison with antiquity.

But the *intension* of gratitude—that is, the degree of obligation to this virtue—is to be judged by how beneficial the favour was to the obligated subject and how unselfishly it was bestowed on him. The minimal degree is to do an *equal* service for the benefactor, if he can receive it (if he is still living) or, if he is dead, to render it to others. [The minimum of gratitude requires one] not to regard a kindness received as a burden one would gladly be rid of (since the person so favoured stands a step lower than his benefactor, and this wounds his pride), but to accept the occasion for gratitude as a moral kindness—that is, an opportunity given one to couple gratitude with love of man, to combine *sensitivity* to others' benevolence (attentiveness to the slightest degree of it in thinking about duty) with the *cordiality* of a benevolent attitude of will, and so to cultivate one's love of man.

124

C. Sympathetic Feeling is a Duty in General
§ 34.

Sympathetic joy and sorrow (*sympathia moralis*) are really sensuous feelings of a pleasure or pain (which should therefore be called aesthetic) at another's state of happiness or sadness (shared feeling, feeling participated in). Nature has already implanted in man the susceptibility for these feelings. But to use this as a means to promoting active and rational benevolence is still a particular, though only a conditioned, duty. It is called the duty of *humanity* (*humanitas*) because it regards man not merely as a rational being but also as an animal endowed with reason. Now humanity can be located either in the *power* and *will* to *share* in others' *feelings* (*humanitas practica*) or merely in the *susceptibility*, given by nature itself, to feel joy and sadness in common with others (*humanitas aesthetica*). The first is *free*, and for this reason it is called a *partaking* (*communio sentiendi liberalis*); it is based on practical reason. [456] The second is *unfree* (*communio sentiendi illiberalis, servilis*); like the communication of warmth or contagious diseases it can be called an *imparting* and also a suffering with another, since it spreads by natural means among men living near one another. It is only to *humanitas practica* that there is an obligation.

The Stoic showed a noble cast of mind when he had his Sage say: I want a friend, not that he might help me in poverty, sickness, imprisonment, *etc.*, but rather that I might stand by him and rescue a man. But the same Sage, when he could not save his friend, said to himself: what is it to me? In other words, he repudiated imparted suffering.

When another person suffers and, although I cannot help him, I let myself be infected by his sorrow (by means of my imagination), then the two of us suffer, though the evil actually (in nature) affects only one. But there cannot possibly be a duty to increase the evil in the world, and so it cannot be a duty to do good from *sympathetic sadness*. This would also be an insulting kind of beneficence, since it expresses benevolence with regard to the unworthy, called *pity*, which has no place in men's relations with one another; for men are not allowed to boast about their worthiness to be happy.

§ 35.

But while it is not in itself a duty to experience sadness, and so also joy, in sympathy with others, it is a duty to participate actively in the fate of others. Hence we have an indirect duty to cultivate the sympathetic natural (aesthetic) feelings in us and to use them as so many means to participating from moral principles and from the feeling appropriate to these principles. —Thus it is our duty: not to avoid places where we shall find the poor who lack the most basic essentials, but rather to seek them out; not to shun sick-rooms or debtors' prisons in order to avoid the painful sympathetic feelings that we cannot guard against. For this is still one of the impulses which nature has implanted in us so that we may do what the thought of duty alone would not accomplish. [457]

Casuistical Questions

Would it not be better for the welfare of the world in general if human morality were limited to juridical duties and these were fulfilled with the utmost conscientiousness, while benevolence were considered morally indifferent? It is not so easy to see what effect this would have on man's happiness. But at least a great moral ornament, love of man,

126

would then be missing from the world. Accordingly benevolence is required for its own sake, in order to present the world in its full perfection as a beautiful moral whole, even if we do not take into account the advantage it brings (in the way of happiness).

Gratitude is not properly mutual love for the benefactor by the man he has put under obligation, but rather *respect* for him. For universal love of one's neighbour can and must be based on equality of duty, whereas in gratitude the one obligated stands a step lower than his benefactor. Is it not this—namely pride—that causes so much ingratitude?—seeing another person above oneself and feeling repugnance at not being able to make oneself fully his equal (so far as relations of duty are concerned)?

On the Vices of Hatred of Man, Which are Directly Opposed (contrarie) *to Love of Man*
§ 36.

They comprise the abominable family of *envy*, *ingratitude*, and *malicious joy* in another's misfortune. —In these vices, however, the hatred is not open and violent but secret and veiled, and this adds baseness to the failure in duty to one's neighbour, so that one also violates duty to oneself.

a) *Envy* (*livor*) is a propensity to view the well-being of others with distress, even though their welfare is in no way detrimental to one's own It is called *qualified envy* when it breaks forth into action (aimed at diminishing their well-being); otherwise it is mere *jealousy* (*invidentia*). Yet envy is only an indirectly malevolent attitude, a reluctance to see our own well-being overshadowed by another's, [which arises] because we know how to value our own well-being and to make this valuation perceptible only in comparison

127

with [458] the well-being of others and not by the standard of its intrinsic worth. —Accordingly we speak, too, of an *enviable* concord and happiness in a marriage or family and so forth, just as if it were permissible, in many cases, to envy someone. The impulses of envy are, therefore, implanted in the nature of man. Only when they break out do they become the abominable vice of a morose and self-torturing obsession which is aimed, at least in one's wishes, at destroying others' good fortune and which is thus contrary to man's duty both to himself and to others.

b) *Ingratitude* toward one's benefactor is called *qualified ingratitude* when it extends to hatred of him; otherwise it is mere *unappreciativeness*. It is, indeed, publicly held to be one of the most detestable vices; and yet man is so notorious for it that we are not surprised if someone makes an enemy by showing kindness. —The ground that makes such a vice possible is a misunderstanding of duty to oneself: the duty of not contracting obligation to others by needing and asking for their beneficence, but rather preferring to bear the hardships of life oneself than to burden others with them and so incur indebtedness (obligation). For we fear that through gratitude we shall have to take the lower place of the dependent in relation to his patron, which is contrary to real self-esteem (pride in the dignity of humanity in one's own person). Hence we freely extend gratitude to those who *necessarily* preceded us in beneficence (to the ancestors we commemorate or to our parents); but to our contemporaries we show gratitude only sparingly and, in fact, even show the opposite of it in order to hide this relation of inequality. —But ingratitude is a vice that rouses humanity to indignation, not merely because of the *harm* that such an example must cause men in general by deterring them from further beneficence (for if their moral attitude is genuine they can, just by disdaining any such return, set all the greater inner moral value on their beneficence), but because ingratitude turns love of man upside down, as it were, and degrades a lack of love into a title to hate the one who does love.

c) *Malicious joy* in another's misfortune, the direct opposite of sympathy, is likewise no stranger to human nature. But when [459] it goes so far as actually to help bring about unhappiness or evil it makes the hatred of men visible and appears in all its hideousness as *qualified malicious joy*. It is indeed natural that, by the laws of imagination (more specifically the law of contrast), we feel our own well-being and even our good conduct more strongly when the misfortune of others or their downfall in scandal is put next to our own good, as a foil to show our good in so much the brighter light. But to take an immediate delight in the existence of such enormities, which destroy the world's highest good, and so also to wish for them to happen, is secretly to hate men; and this is the direct contrary of love for our neighbour, which is incumbent on us as duty. It is the *haughtiness* of others when their welfare is uninterrupted, and their *pride* in their good conduct (but really only in their good fortune in having so far escaped temptations to public vice)—both of which the self-loving man imputes to himself as merit—that generate this fiendish joy, which is diametrically opposed to our duty according to the principle of sympathy (as expressed by Terence's noble Chremes): "I am a man; whatever befalls man concerns me too."

The sweetest form of this malicious joy is *revengefulness*. Besides, it even looks as if one had the supreme right and even the obligation (as a thirst for justice) to make the misfortune of others one's end even without any advantage to oneself.

Every deed that offends a man's right deserves punishment, the function of which is to *avenge* the crime upon its perpetrator (not merely to make good the injury). But punishment is not a function which the injured party can undertake on his private authority, but rather the function of a tribunal distinct from him, which gives effect to the law of a *supreme authority* over all those subject to him; and if (as we must do in ethics) we regard men as in a juridical state, although under mere *laws of reason* (not civil laws), then no one has the moral title to inflict punishment and to avenge the injuries sustained by men except Him who is also the supreme moral lawgiver; and He alone (namely God) can say: "Vengeance is mine; I will repay." It is, therefore, a duty of virtue not only to refrain from repaying another's enmity with hatred out of mere revenge but also never even to call upon the world-judge for vengeance—partly because a man has enough guilt of his own to be greatly in need of forgiveness [460] and partly, and indeed especially, because no punishment, no matter from whom it comes, may be inflicted out of hatred. —Hence men have a duty to cultivate a *conciliatory spirit* (*placabilitas*). But this must not be confused with *placid toleration* of injuries (*mitis iniuriarum patientia*), renunciation of the rigorous means (*rigorosa*) for preventing the recurrence of injuries by other men; for in the latter case a man would be throwing away his right and letting others trample on it, and so would violate his duty to himself.

Note

If we take vice in the sense of a basic principle (a qualified vice), then any vice which would make human nature itself detestable is *inhuman*, from an objective point of view. But considered subjectively—that is, from what experience teaches us about our species—such vices are still *human*. As to whether, in the vehemence of aversion, one could call some of these vices *devilish* and, similarly, the virtues opposed to them *angelic*, both of these notions are only Ideas of a maximum, conceived as a standard for the sake of comparing degrees of morality; in them one assigns man his place in *heaven* or *hell*, without making of him an intermediate sort of being who occupies neither one place nor the other. The question may remain open here whether Haller did not hit upon it better with his "an ambiguous something intermediate between the angels and the brutes." But the bisection of a being composed of heterogeneous elements really produces no determinate concept, and nothing can bring us to such a concept if we try to order beings whose class distinctions are unknown to us. The first comparison (of angelic virtue and devilish vice) is an exaggeration. The second—although men do, alas, fall into *brutish* vice—does not justify our attributing to them a disposition *characteristic of their species*, any more than the stunting of some trees in the forest is a reason for making them a special *kind* of plant. [461]

SECTION II. ON DUTIES OF VIRTUE TO OTHER MEN
WHICH ARISE FROM THE *respect* DUE TO THEM

§ 37.

Moderation in one's demands generally—that is, the willing limitation of one man's self-love by the self-love of others—is called *modesty*. Want of such moderation (lack of modesty) in one's claims to be *loved* by others is called *egotism* (*philautia*). But lack of modesty in one's claims to *respect* from others is self-*conceit* (*arrogantia*). The *respect* that I bear for others or that another can claim from me (*observantia aliis praestanda*) is therefore the recognition of a *dignity* (*dignitas*) in other men, *i.e.* of a worth that has no price or no equivalent for which the object of esteem (*aestimii*) could be exchanged. —The assessment of anything as worthless is contempt.

§ 38.

Every man has a rightful claim to *respect* from his fellow-men and is *reciprocally* obligated to show respect for every other man.

Humanity itself is a dignity; for man cannot be used merely as a means by any man (either by others or even by himself) but must always be treated at the same time as an end. And it is just this that comprises his dignity (personality), by virtue of which he assumes superiority over all the other beings in the world which are not men and can be used—hence over all *things*. But just as he cannot give himself away for any price (this would conflict with his duty to himself), so neither can he act contrary to the equally necessary self-esteem in which others, as men, hold themselves; in other words, he is obligated to acknowledge, in a practical way, the dignity of humanity in every other man. Hence he is subject to a duty based on the respect which he must show every other man. [462]

§ 39.

To *despise* others (*contemnere*)—that is, to deny them the respect due to men as such—is in any case contrary to duty; for they are men. One cannot, it is true, help *disdaining* some of them inwardly in comparison with others (*despicatui habere*); but the outward manifestation of disdain is, nevertheless, an affront. —What is *dangerous* is no object of contempt, and so neither is the immoral man; and if my superiority to his attacks entitles me to say: I despise that man, this means nothing more than: I am in no danger from him even though I have prepared no defence against him, because he shows himself in all his vileness. Nonetheless I cannot deny all respect to even the immoral man as a man; I cannot withdraw at least the respect that belongs to him in his quality as a man, even though by his deed he makes himself unworthy of his humanity. Thus there can be disgraceful punishments which dishonour humanity itself (such as quartering a man, having him torn by dogs, cutting off his nose and ears). To the honour-loving man (who, as everyone must do, lays claim to respect from others) these punishments are more grievous than loss of property and life; moreover they make the spectator blush with shame at belonging to a species that can be used in such a way.

Note

On this there is based a duty of respect for man even in the logical use of his reason: a duty not to censure his error by calling it absurdity, poor judgment and so forth, but rather to suppose that his error must yet contain some truth and to seek this out, uncovering, at the same time, the deceptive appearance (the subjective determining ground of judgment which, by an oversight, he took for the objective), and so, by explaining to him the possibility of his having erred, to preserve his respect for his own reason. For if, by such expressions, we deny all understanding to the man who opposes us in a certain opinion, how can we make him understand that he has erred in it? —The same thing applies to the censure of vice, which must never break out into complete contempt and denial of all moral worth to the immoral man;

for on this supposition he could [463] never be improved, and this is not consistent with the Idea of *man*, who as such (as a moral being) can never lose all his disposition to the good.

§ 40.

Reverence for the law, which on the side of the subject can be designated as moral feeling, is one with man's consciousness of his duty. For the same reason, display of respect before man as a moral being (one holding his duty in highest esteem) is itself a duty which others have toward him and [on his part] a right to which he cannot renounce the claim. —This claim is called *love of honour*, which manifests itself in outward conduct as *rectitude* (*honestas externa*); the violation of it is called *scandal*, an example of disregard for it which might lead others to follow the example. To *give* scandal is in the highest degree contrary to duty. But to *find* scandal in what is merely paradoxical (*paradoxon*), but otherwise good in itself, is a delusion (since one confuses the unusual with the impermissible) and an error which tends to endanger and corrupt virtue. —For in giving an example of due respect for others we cannot degenerate into blind imitation (in which custom, *mos*, is raised to the dignity of a law)—a tyranny of popular mores which would be contrary to man's duty to himself.

§ 41.

To neglect mere duties of love is *lack of virtue* (*peccatum*). But to neglect duty that proceeds from the *respect* due to every man as such is *vice* (*vitium*). For no one is wronged when we neglect duties of love; but if we fail in a duty of respect, then a man is deprived of his lawful claim. —The first transgression is opposed to duty as a *contrary* (*contrarie oppositum virtutis*). But [violation of a duty of respect] is not only a want of moral embellishment; it even removes the value of the respect that would otherwise *stand* the subject *in good stead*, and is therefore *vice*.

For this reason, too, duties to one's fellow-men which arise from the respect due them are expressed only negatively; this [464] duty of virtue, in other words, is expressed only indirectly (by the prohibition of the opposite).

On the Vices Which Violate Duties of Respect for Other Men

These vices are a) *pride*, b) *calumny*, and c) *mockery*.

A. Pride

§ 42.

Pride (*superbia* and, as this word expresses it, the desire to be always on top) is a kind of *ambition* (*ambitio*) in which we demand that others think little of themselves in comparison with us. It is, therefore, a vice opposed to the respect which every man can rightfully claim.

It is distinguished from proper pride (*animus elatus*), which is *love of honour*, *i.e.* anxiety to yield nothing of one's human dignity in comparison with others (which pride we often characterize with the epithet "*noble*"); for pride [as ambition] demands from others a respect which it denies them. —But even this [proper] pride becomes a fault and an affront when it, too, is merely a demand upon others to concern themselves with our importance.

Pride is, as it were, a solicitation on the part of the ambitious man for followers, whom he thinks he is entitled to treat contemptuously. It is clear of itself that this is *unjust* and opposed to the respect due to men as such; that it is *folly*—that is, foolishness in using the means to something which, in this connection, is not worth being taken as an end; that it is, in fact, even *stupidity*—that is, an offensive want of understanding in using such means as must bring about, on the part of other men, the exact opposite of one's end (for the more the ambitious man shows that he is trying to obtain respect, the more everyone denies it to him). But it might not [465] be noticed that the ambitious man is always *abject* in the depths of his soul. For he would not demand that others think little of themselves in comparison with him unless he knew that, were his fortune suddenly to change, he himself would not find it very hard to grovel and to waive any claim to respect from others.

B. Calumny
§ 43.

By *calumny* (*obtrectatio*) or backbiting I do not mean *slander* (*contumelia*), *false* defamation to be taken to Law; I mean merely the immediate inclination, with no particular end in view, to bring into the open something prejudicial to respect for others. This is contrary to the respect due to humanity as such; for the scandal so given weakens this respect, on which the impulse to the morally good rests, and so far as possible makes people sceptical about it.

The wilful *spreading* (*propalatio*) of something that detracts from another person's honour—even if it does not come under the jurisdiction of the courts and even if what is said is true—diminishes respect for humanity as such, so as finally to cast the shadow of worthlessness over our race itself, making misanthropy (aversion from men) or contempt the prevalent way of thinking, or to dull our moral feeling by repeatedly exposing us to the sight of men's faults and accustoming us to it. It is, therefore, a duty of virtue not to take a malicious delight in exposing the faults of others so that people will think we are as good as, or at least not worse than, other men, but rather to throw the veil of benevolence over their faults, not merely by softening our judgments but also by keeping these judgments to ourselves; for the example of respect which we give others can arouse their striving to deserve it. For this reason even anthropology's prying into the morals of others (*allotrioepiscopia*) is already an offensive inquisitiveness and impertinence which anyone can rightfully resist as a violation of the respect due to him. [466]

C. Mockery
§ 44.

Wanton censure and a mania for ridicule, the propensity to expose others to laughter so as to make their faults the immediate object of our amusement, are [a form of] malice. They are altogether different from *banter*, familiarity among friends which consists in laughing at their peculiarities only as if they were faults, but really as departures from the rule of fashion which are the prerogative of courage (for this is not at all *scornful laughter*). But to expose to laughter real faults which would tend to rob the person of the respect he deserves, or supposed faults as if they were real, has something of fiendish delight in it, as does the propensity to this, a *caustic wit* (*spiritus causticus*); and this makes it an even more serious violation of our duty of respect to other men.

This must be distinguished from repelling contemptuously, in a joking but still derisive way, the insulting attack of an adversary, by which rejoinder (*retorsio iocosa*)

THE DOCTRINE OF VIRTUE

the mocker (or, in general, a malicious but ineffectual adversary) is similarly ridiculed. This is a rightful defence of the respect we can require from that adversary. But when the object of his ridicule is really not a topic for wit, but one in which reason necessarily takes a moral interest, then no matter how much ridicule our adversary may have uttered and no matter how much he may have exposed us to laughter by it, it is more befitting the dignity of the topic either to put up no defence against the attack or to conduct the defence with dignity and seriousness.

Note

It will be noticed that under the heading above [Duties of Respect] we do not so much commend virtues as rather censure the vices opposed to them. But that is already implicit in the concept of the respect we are obligated to show other men, which is only a *negative* duty. —I am not obligated to *honour* others (regarded merely as men)—that is, to show them *positive* high esteem. The only reverence to which I am naturally obligated is reverence for the law [467] as such (*reverere legem*); and to reverence the law is man's universal and unconditioned duty to others, which each of them can demand as the respect originally due him (*observantia debita*).²⁵ But it is not a duty to hold other men as such in honour (*reverentia adversus hominem*) or to give them some service in this way.

The various forms of respect to be shown to others according to their different circumstances or the contingent relations of men—differences of age, sex, birth, strength or weakness, or even station and dignity, which depend in part on arbitrary decrees—cannot be set forth in detail and classified in the *metaphysical* first principles of the doctrine of virtue, since here we have to do only with its pure principles of reason.

§ *45.*

These (duties of virtue) do not really call for a special chapter in the system of pure ethics; since they are not principles of obligation for men as such to one another, they cannot really comprise a part of the *metaphysical* first principles of the doctrine of virtue. They are only rules modified according to the differences of the subjects to whom we *apply* the principle of virtue (on its formal side) in cases that arise in experience (the material). Hence, like anything divided on an empirical basis, they do not admit of a classification that could be guaranteed to be complete. Nevertheless, just as we need a passage from the metaphysic of nature to physics—a transition which has its own special rules—so we rightly demand something similar from the metaphysic of morals: a transition which, by applying the pure principles of duty to cases of experience, would *schematize* these principles, as it were, and present them as ready for morally-practical use.—How should one behave, for example, to men who are morally pure or depraved? to the cultivated or the crude? to the [468] learned or the ignorant and, among the learned, to those who handle their science in a sociable (polished) way or in a specialized (pedantic) way—to those who aim at practical goals or rather at wit and taste? How should men be treated by virtue of their differences in rank, age, sex, health, prosperity or poverty and so forth?

These questions do not yield so many different *kinds* of ethical *obligation* (for there is only *one* kind—that of virtue as such), but only so many different *ways of applying* [the one principle of virtue] (corollaries). Hence they cannot be presented as parts of ethics and members of the *division* of a system (which must proceed *a priori* from a concept of reason). They can only be appended to the system. —But even this application belongs to the complete exposition of the system.

CONCLUSION OF THE DOCTRINE OF ELEMENTS

On the Intimate Union of Love and Respect in Friendship
§ *46.*

Friendship (considered in its perfection) is the union of two persons through equal and mutual love and respect. —It is easy to see that [perfect friendship] is an ideal of the emotional and practical concern which each of the friends united through a morally good will takes in the other's welfare; and even if friendship does not produce the complete happiness of life, the adoption of this ideal in men's attitude to one another contains their worthiness to be happy. Hence men have a duty of friendship. —The striving for perfect friendship (as the maximum good in the attitude of friends to each other) is a duty imposed by reason—not, indeed, an ordinary duty but a duty of honour. Yet it is easy to see that [perfect] friendship is a mere Idea (although a practically necessary one), which cannot be achieved in practice. For in his relations with his neighbour how can a man ascertain whether one of the attitudes essential to this duty (*e.g.* mutual benevolence) is *equal* on the part of both friends? Or, still more important, how can he be sure what relation exists, in the

140

same person, between the feeling connected with the one duty and that connected with the other (*e.g.* between the feeling connected with benevolence and that connected with respect)? And how can he be sure that if one of the friends [469] is more ardent in his *love* he may not, just because of this, forfeit something of the other's *respect?* Does not all this mean that love and respect on the part of both friends can hardly be brought subjectively into that balanced proportion which is yet necessary for friendship? —For we can regard love as attraction and respect as repulsion, and if the principle of love commands friends to come together, the principle of respect requires them to keep each other at a proper distance. This limitation upon intimacy, which is expressed in the rule that even the best of friends should not make themselves *too familiar* with each other, contains a maxim which holds not only for the superior in relation to the inferior but also vice-versa. For if the superior suddenly feels his pride wounded, he may want the inferior's respect to be put aside for the moment, but not abolished. But once respect is violated, its presence within is irrevocably lost, even though the outward marks of it (manners) are brought back to their former course.

Friendship conceived as attainable in its purity or completeness (between Orestes and Pylades, Theseus and Pirithous) is the hobby horse of writers of romance. On the other hand Aristotle says: My dear friends, there is no such thing as a friend! The following remarks may point up the difficulties in perfect friendship.

From a moral point of view it is, of course, a duty for one of the friends to point out the other's faults to him; this is in the other's best interests and is therefore a duty of love. But his *alter ego* sees in this a lack of the respect which he expected from his friend and thinks either that he has already lost something of his friend's respect or that, since he is observed and secretly criticized, he is in constant danger of losing it; and even the fact that his friend observes him and finds fault with him will seem in itself an insult.

How we wish for a friend in need—one who is, of course, an active friend, ready to help us at his own expense! But still it is also a heavy burden to feel chained to another's fate and encumbered with his needs. —Hence friendship cannot be a union aimed at mutual advantage: the union must rather be a pure moral one, and the help that each of the two may count on from the other in case of need must not be regarded as the end and motive of friendship—for in that case he would lose the other's respect—but only as the [470] outward manifestation of an inner heartfelt benevolence, which should not be put to the test since this is always dangerous. Each friend is generously concerned with sparing the other his burden and bearing it all by himself, even concealing it altogether from his friend, while yet he can always flatter himself that in case of need he could confidently count on the other's help. But if one of them accepts a *favour* from the other, then he may well be able to count on equality in love, but not in respect; for he sees himself obviously a step lower in so far as he is under obligation without being able reciprocally to impose obligation.—It is sweet to feel a mutual possession that approximates to a fusion into one person. Yet friendship is something so *delicate* (*teneritas amicitiae*) that it is never for a moment safe from *interruptions* if it is allowed to rest on feelings and if this mutual sympathy and self-surrender are not subjected to principles or rules preventing excessive familiarity and limiting mutual love by the requirements of respect. Such interruptions are common among uncultivated people, although they do not always result in a *split* (for the rabble fight and make up). These people cannot part with each other, and yet they cannot come to terms with each other since they need quarrels in order to savour the sweetness of being united in reconciliation. —But in any case the love in friendship cannot be an *agitation* [*Affekt*]: for this is blind in its choice, and after a while it goes up in smoke.

§ 47.

Moral friendship (as distinguished from emotional friendship) is the complete confidence of two persons in revealing their secret thoughts and feelings to each other, in so far as such disclosures are consistent with mutual respect for each other.

Man is a being meant for society (though he is also an unsociable one), and in cultivating social intercourse he feels strongly the need to reveal himself to others (even with no ulterior purpose). But on the other hand, hemmed in and cautioned by fear of the misuse others may make of this disclosure of his thoughts, he finds himself constrained [471] to *lock up* in himself a good part of his opinions (especially those about other people). He would like to discuss with someone his opinions about his associates the government, religion and so forth, but he cannot risk it —partly because the other person, while prudently keeping back his own opinions, might use this to harm him, and partly because, if he revealed his failings while the other person concealed his own, he would lose something of the other's respect by presenting himself quite candidly to him.

[471]

If he finds someone understanding—someone who, moreover, shares his general outlook on things—with whom he need not be anxious about this danger but can reveal himself with complete confidence, he can then air his views. He is not completely *alone* with his thoughts, as in a prison, but enjoys a freedom denied to him with the rank and file, with whom he must shut himself up in himself. Every man has his secrets and dare not confide blindly in others, partly because most men have a base disposition to use these secrets to his prejudice and partly because many people are indiscreet or incapable of judging and distinguishing what may or may not be repeated. The necessary combination of qualities is seldom found in one person (*rara avis in terris, nigroque simillima cygno*[27]), especially since the closest friendship requires that this understanding and trusted friend be also bound not to share the secrets entrusted to him with anyone else, no matter how reliable he thinks him, without explicit permission to do so.

This (merely moral) friendship is not just an ideal but (like the black swan) actually exists here and there in its perfection. But (pragmatic) friendship, which burdens itself with the ends of other men, although out of love, can have neither the purity nor the completeness requisite for a maxim which determines actions precisely: it is an ideal of our wishes, which knows no bounds in the concept of pure reason but which must always be very limited in experience.

A *friend of man* as such (that is, of the whole race) is one who sympathizes emotionally with the welfare of all men (shares their delight in it) and will never disturb it without heartfelt regret. Yet the expression "a *friend* of man" is somewhat narrower in its meaning than "one who merely loves man" (a *philanthropist*). For [472] "a friend of man" contains thought and consideration for the *equality* among men, and hence the Idea that in obligating others by his beneficence he is himself obligated, as if all men are brothers under one universal father who wills the happiness of all. —For the relation of a patron, as a benefactor, to the man he patronizes, as one obligated to gratitude, is indeed a relation of mutual love, but not of friendship, since the respect which the two owe each other is not equal. The duty of practicing benevolence as a friend of man (a necessary humbling of oneself), if it is reflected upon, serves to guard against the pride which usually comes over those fortunate enough to have the means for beneficence.

Appendix
§ 48.
On the Virtues of Social Intercourse (virtutes homileticae)

It is a duty both to ourselves and to others not to *isolate* ourselves (*separatistam agere*) but to bring our moral perfection into social intercourse (*officium commercii, sociabilitas*); while we should make ourselves a fixed center of our principles, we should regard the circle thus drawn around us as one that also forms a part of the all-inclusive circle of those who, in their attitude, are citizens of the world. The end in this duty is not to promote the highest good of the world but only the means that lead indirectly to this end—means such as pleasantness in our relations with others, good-naturedness, mutual love and respect (affability and propriety, *humanitas aesthetica et decorum*). By this we associate virtue with the graces, and to effect this is in itself a duty of virtue.

These are, indeed, only *outworks* or by-products

(*parerga*), which present a fair illusion of something like virtue, an illusion which also deceives no one, since everyone knows how to take it. *Affability, sociability, courtesy, hospitality,* and *gentleness* (in disagreeing without quarreling) are, indeed, only small change; yet they promote the feeling for virtue itself by [arousing] a striving to bring this illusion as near as possible to the truth. All of these, [473] like the mere manners of social intercourse, manifest what is obligatory and also bind others to it; and in so doing they work toward a virtuous attitude in so far as they at least make virtue *fashionable.*

But the question arises here whether we may also keep company with the vicious. We cannot avoid meeting them, unless we leave the world; and besides, our judgment about them is not competent. —But if the vice is a scandal —that is, a publicly given example of contempt for the strict laws of duty, which therefore brings infamy with it —then even if the laws of the country do not punish the vice, we must break off the existing association or avoid it as much as possible. For the further continuation of it does away with all the honour of virtue and puts it up for sale to anyone who is rich enough to bribe parasites with the pleasures of luxury. [474]

II

THE ETHICAL DOCTRINE OF METHOD

ETHICAL DIDACTIC

§ *49.*

Although virtue cannot be based on anthropological knowledge drawn from experience, the very concept of virtue implies that virtue must be acquired (that it is not innate). For man's capacity for moral action would not be virtue were it not produced by the *strength* of his resolution struggling with such powerful inclinations to the contrary. Virtue is the product of pure practical reason, in so far as reason, aware of its supremacy (on grounds of freedom), wins ascendancy over the inclinations.

That virtue can and must be *learned* follows directly from the fact that it is not innate. The theory of virtue is, therefore, a *doctrine*. But one does not, merely by the theory of how one should behave in keeping with the concept of virtue, acquire the strength to put the rule into practice. Hence the Stoics [in denying that virtue can be learned] meant only that virtue cannot be *learned* through the mere presentation of duty or through admonitions, but must rather be cultivated (by discipline) and *practiced* by being put to the proof of combat with the inner enemy in man; for one *cannot* straightway do all that one *wills* to do, without having first tried and practiced one's strength. But the *resolution* to practice virtue must be made all at once and in its entirety, since the intention (*animus*) of surrendering at times to vice, in order gradually to break away from it, would in itself be impure and even immoral. Consequently this attitude could also produce no virtue (in so far as virtue is based on a single principle). [477]

§ *50.*

Now as for the doctrinal method (and *methodic* treatment is essential to any scientific doctrine—otherwise the exposition of it would be chaotic), this too must be systematic and not fragmentary if the doctrine of virtue is to present itself as a science. —But the doctrine can be delivered either in a *lecture*, as when all those to whom it is directed are a mere audience, or by the method of *questioning*, in which the teacher asks his pupil what he wants to teach him. And this method of questioning is, in turn, divided into the method of *dialogue* and that of *catechism*, depending on whether the teacher addresses his questions to the pupil's *reason* or merely to his *memory*. For if the teacher wants to question his pupil's reason he must do this in a dialogue in which teacher and pupil reciprocally question and answer each other. The teacher, by his questions, guides the pupil's thinking merely by presenting him with situations in which his disposition for certain concepts will develop (the teacher is the midwife of the pupil's thoughts). The pupil, who thus sees that he is able to think for himself, provides, by his questions about obscurities or doubts in the propositions admitted, occasion for the *teacher* to *learn* how to question skilfully, according to the saying *docendo discimus*. —(For logic has not yet taken sufficiently to heart its task of furnishing us with rules as to the appropriate way of searching for things: that is to say, logic should not limit itself to giving rules for *determinant* judgments but should also provide rules for *preparatory* judgments (*iudicia praevia*), by which one is led to conceptions. Such a doctrine can be a guide even to the mathematician in his inventions, and moreover he often makes use of it.)

§ *51.*

For the still untrained pupil the first and most essential *doctrinal* instrument of the theory of virtue is a moral *catechism*. This must precede the religious catechism. It cannot be interwoven, as a mere interpolation, in the teachings of religion but must rather be presented separately, as a self-subsistent whole. For it is only by pure moral principles that the transition from the doctrine of virtue to religion can be made, since otherwise the avowals of religion would be impure. —For their own part, even the worthiest and most eminent theologians [478] have hesitated to draw up a catechism for statutory religion which they would personally answer for, although one would have thought this the least that could be expected from the vast treasury of their learning.

But a *moral* catechism, the basic teaching of the doctrine of virtue, involves no such scruple or difficulty since, so far as its content is concerned, it can be developed from ordinary human reason and, so far as its form is concerned, it needs only to be adapted to the didactic rules appropriate to the earliest instruction. The formal principle of such instruction does not, however, permit Socratic *dialogue* as the method of teaching, since the pupil has no idea what questions to ask; and so the teacher alone does the questioning. But the answer which he methodically draws from the pupil's reason must be written down and preserved in precise terms which cannot easily be altered, and so be committed to the pupil's *memory*. In this way the *catechetical method* differs from both the *dogmatic method* (in which only the teacher speaks) and the *method of dialogue* (in which both teacher and pupil question and answer each other).

§ 52.

The *experimental* (technical) means to the formation of virtue is *good example* on the part of the teacher (his exemplary conduct) and *cautionary* example in others. For, to the as yet unformed human being, imitation is what first determines him to embrace the maxims that he afterwards makes his own. —To become conditioned to something is to establish a permanent inclination apart from any maxim, by the often repeated satisfaction of that inclination; it is a mechanism of sense rather than a principle of thought (and one that is easier to *make* than to *break* after it has been acquired). —As for the power of *examples** (good or bad) which can be held up to the propensity for imitation or presented as warnings [479], what is given to us by others can establish no maxim of virtue. For a maxim of virtue consists precisely in the subjective autonomy of each man's practical reason, and so implies that the law itself, not the conduct of other men, serves as one's motive. Thus the teacher will not tell his pupil "Take an example from that good (orderly, diligent) boy!" For this would only cause the pupil to hate that boy, who puts him in an unfavorable light. Good example (exemplary conduct) should not serve as a model but only as a proof that it is really possible to act in accordance with duty. Thus it is not comparison with any other man what-

---

* The German words "instance [*Beispiel*]" and "example [*Exempel*]", though commonly used as synonyms, do not really have exactly the same meaning. To take an *example* of something and to bring forward an *instance* to clarify a term are altogether different concepts. An example is a particular case of a *practical* rule, in so far as this demonstrates the feasibility or impracticability of an action, whereas an *instance* is only the particular (*concretum*), presented as contained under the general by means of concepts (*abstractum*), and is merely a theoretical illustration of a concept.

[479]

soever (with men as they are), but comparison with the Idea of humanity (with what man ought to be) and so with the law, that must serve as the constant standard of the teacher's instruction.

Note
Fragments of a Moral Catechism

The teacher questions the pupil's reason about what he wants to teach him; and should the pupil sometimes not know how to answer the question, the teacher, guiding his reason, suggests the answer.

1. Teacher: What is your greatest, in fact your whole, desire in life?

   Pupil: (is silent)

   Teacher: That everything should always go the way you want it to.

2. Teacher: What do we call such a state?

   Pupil: (is silent)

   Teacher: We call it *happiness* (continuous well-being, enjoyment of life, complete contentment with one's state).

3. Teacher: Now if it were up to you to dispose of all the happiness possible in the world, would you keep it all for yourself or would you share it with your fellow-men?

   Pupil: I would share it with others and make them happy and contented too.

4. Teacher: Now that shows that you have a good enough *heart;* but let us see whether you show good *under-standing* along with it. —Would you really [480] give the lazy fellow a soft cushion so that he could pass away his life in sweet idleness? Or would you see to it that the drunkard is never short of wine

and whatever else he needs to get drunk? Would you give the swindler a charming air and manner to dupe other people? And would you give the brutal man audacity and strong fists so that he could crush other people? Each of these things is a means that somebody wants in order to be happy in his own way.

Pupil: No, I would not.

5. Teacher: You see, then, that if you had all happiness in your hands and, along with it, the best will, you still would not straightway give it to anyone who put out his hand for it; instead you would first try to find out to what extent each is *worthy* of happiness. —But as for yourself, would you at least have no scruples about first giving yourself everything that you count in your happiness?

Pupil: I would have none.

Teacher: But doesn't it occur to you to ask, again, whether you yourself are worthy of happiness?

Pupil: Of course.

Teacher: Now the force in you that strives only toward happiness is *inclination;* but the power that limits your inclination to the condition of your first being worthy of happiness is your *reason;* and your power to restrain and overcome your inclination by your reason is the freedom of your will.

6. Teacher: As to how you should set about participating in happiness and also becoming at least not unworthy of it, the rule and instruction in this lies in your *reason* alone. This means that you need not learn this rule for your conduct from experience or be taught it by other men. Your own reason teaches you what you have to do and directly commands

it. For example, suppose a situation in which you could get a great benefit for yourself or your friends by making up a little lie that would harm no one: what does your reason say about it?

Pupil: That I ought not to lie, no matter how great the benefits to myself and my friend might be. Lying is *base* and makes a man *unworthy* of happiness. — Here we find an unconditional necessitation through a command (or prohibition) of reason, which I must obey; and in the face of it all my inclinations must be silent.

Teacher: What do we call this necessity, which reason lays directly upon a man, [481] of acting in conformity with a law of reason?

Pupil: It is called *duty*.

Teacher: So a man's fulfillment of his duty is the universal and sole condition of his worthiness to be happy, and his fulfillment of duty is one with his worthiness to be happy.

7. Teacher: But even if we are conscious of a good and active will in us, by virtue of which we consider ourselves worthy (or at least not unworthy) of happiness, can we base on this the sure hope of participating in happiness?

Pupil: No, not merely on this. For it is not always within our power to make ourselves happy, and the course of nature does not of itself conform with merit. Our happiness in life (our welfare in general) depends, rather, on circumstances that, by and large, are not under man's control. So our happiness always remains a mere wish which cannot become a hope unless some other power is added.

8. Teacher: Has reason, in fact, grounds for admitting

the reality of such a power, which apportions happiness according to man's merit or guilt—a power ordering the whole of nature and ruling the world with supreme wisdom?

Pupil: Yes. For we see in the works of nature, which we can judge, a wisdom so widespread and profound that we can explain it to ourselves only by the ineffably great art of a creator of the world. And from this we have cause, when we turn to the moral order, which is the highest adornment of the world, to expect there a rule no less wise. In other words, we have cause to hold that if we do not make ourselves *unworthy of happiness* by violating our duty, we can also hope to *share* in happiness.

In this catechism, which must be carried through all the articles of virtue and vice, the greatest care must be taken *not* to base the command of duty on the fact that it is actually observed by the men it is supposed to obligate nor even on the advantage or detriment to others flowing from it. It must rather be based quite purely on the moral principle, and only casual mention should be made of advantage and detriment, as of an adjunct which could really be dispensed with but which is serviceable, as a mere instrument, for the taste of those who are [482] weak by nature. It is the *shamefulness* of vice, not its *harmfulness* (to the agent himself), that must be emphasized above all. For unless the dignity of virtue is exalted above everything else in actions, then the concept of duty itself vanishes and dissolves into mere pragmatic precepts, since man's consciousness of his own nobility then disappears and he is for sale and can be bought for a price that the seductive inclinations offer him.

Now when this is wisely and carefully developed out of

156   [482]

man's own reason, with regard for the differences in age, sex, and position which he gradually encounters, then at the end there must be something more—something that moves the soul inwardly and puts man in a position such that he can look upon himself only with the greatest wonder at the original disposition dwelling in him, the impression of which is never erased. When at the end of his instruction he once more, by way of summary, recounts his duties in their order (recapitulates them); and when, in the case of each of them, his attention is drawn to the fact that none of the pains, hardships, and sufferings of life—not even the threat of death—which may befall him because he attends faithfully to his duty can make him lose his consciousness of being their master and superior to them all; then it is time for the question: what is it in you that can be trusted to enter into combat with all the powers of nature in you and around you and, if they come into conflict with your moral principles, to conquer them? Although the answer to this question completely surpasses the power of speculative reason, the question arises of itself. And if he takes it to heart, the very incomprehensibility of this self-knowledge must produce an exaltation in his soul which only inspires it the more to keep its duty holy, the more it is assailed.

In this catechetical instruction in morality it would be most helpful to the pupil's moral development to raise some casuistical questions in the analysis of every duty and to let the assembled children put their reason to the test of how each would go about resolving the tricky problem put before him. The advantage of this is not only that, as a method of [483] *cultivating reason*, casuistry is most suitable to the capacity of the undeveloped (since questions about duty can be decided far more easily than

[483]

speculative questions), and so is the most appropriate way to sharpen the reason of young people in general. Its advantage lies especially in the fact that it is natural for man to *love* a subject which he has, by his own handling, brought to a science (in which he is now proficient); and so, by this sort of practice, the pupil is drawn unwittingly to an *interest* in morality.

But it is of foremost importance in this instruction not to present the moral catechism mixed with the religious one (to combine them into one) or, what is worse yet, to let it follow upon the religious catechism. On the contrary, the pupil must always be brought to a clear insight into the moral catechism, which should be presented with the greatest diligence and completeness. For otherwise the religion that the pupil afterwards professes will be nothing but hypocrisy: he will embrace duties out of fear and feign an interest in them which is not in his heart.

SECTION II. ETHICAL ASCETIC

§ 53.

The rules for practicing virtue (*exercitiorum virtutis*) aim at a frame of mind that is *brave* and *cheerful* in the observance of duty (*animus strenuus et hilaris*). For in order to overcome the obstacles with which it has to contend, virtue must collect all its strength and at the same time sacrifice many of the pleasures of life, the loss of which can well make the mind morose and surly at times. But what we do cheerlessly and merely as compulsory service has no intrinsic value for us, and so also if we attend to our duty in this way; we do not love it but rather shirk as much as we can the occasion for practicing it.

The cultivation of virtue, *i.e.* moral *asceticism*, takes as its motto for the vigorous, spirited, and courageous practice of virtue the *Stoic* saying: accustom yourself *to bear* the contingent ills of life and *to do without* the equally superfluous pleasures (*assuesce incommodis et desuesce commoditatibus vitae*). It is a [484] kind of *hygiene* that man should practice to keep himself morally *healthy*. But health is only the *negative* side of well-being: it cannot itself be felt. Something must be added to it—something which, though it is purely moral, offers a pleasant enjoyment of life—and this is the habitually cheerful heart, as the virtuous *Epicurus* conceived it. For who should have more cause for a cheerful spirit, without finding it his duty to acquire such a frame of mind and make it habitual, than the man who is aware of no intentional transgression in himself and is secured against falling into such a transgression? (*hic murus aheneus esto etc., Horat.*) On the other hand monastic asceticism, which, out of superstitious fear or hypocritical self-loathing, goes to work with self-torture and crucifixion of the flesh, does not aim at virtue but rather at fantastic atonement; it inflicts self-punishment and, instead of requiring moral *repentance* for a fault (that is, repentance with a view to self-improvement) insists on *penance* for it. But a self-chosen and self-inflicted punishment is a contradiction (because punishment must always be inflicted by another person); moreover it cannot produce the cheerfulness that accompanies virtue, but much rather brings with it secret hatred for virtue's command. —Ethical gymnastic, therefore, consists only in combatting the impulses of nature to the extent that we are able to master them when a situation comes up in which they threaten morality; hence it is a combat which gives us courage and makes us cheerful in the consciousness of our restored freedom. To *repent* of something and to impose a *penance* on oneself (for example, a fast) not

[484]   159

from hygienic but from pious considerations are, morally considered, two very different precautionary measures. To repent of a past transgression when we recall it is inevitable and, in fact, we even have a duty not to let this recollection atrophy; but self-punishment, which is cheerless, morose, and surly, makes virtue itself hated and drives away its followers. Hence the training (discipline) which man exercises on himself can become meritorious and exemplary only by the cheerfulness that accompanies it. [485]

The Doctrine of Religion, as the Doctrine of Duties to God, Lies Beyond the Bounds of Pure Moral Philosophy

Protagoras of Abdera began his book with the words: *"As for whether the gods exist or not, I have nothing to say."** For this the Athenians expelled him from the city and from the land he owned and burned his books before the public assembly. (*Quinctiliani Inst. Orat. lib.*3 *cap.*1)[28] —In doing this, the Athenian judges, as *men*, behaved most *unjustly* to him; but as *state officials* and judges they proceeded quite *justly* and consequently; for how could a man swear an oath unless it were decreed publicly and as law, *by order of the sovereign authorities (de par le Sénat)*, that gods exist?** [486]

But, granting these beliefs and admitting that the *doctrine of religion* is an integral part of the general *doctrine*

---

* *"De diis, neque ut sint, neque ut non sint, habeo dicere."*
** Later on, however, a great sage completely forbade, from the viewpoint of moral legislation, the taking of oaths as something nonsensical and, at the same time, almost bordering on blasphemy. But from a political point of view people still maintain that this mechanism is quite indispensable as a means serving the administration of public justice, and liberal interpretations of that prohibition have been thought up in order to soften it. —But, since it would be absurd to swear in earnest that God exists (because one must already have postulated this in order to be able to take an oath at all), the question still remains: whether an oath would not be possible and valid if one swears only *in case* God may exist (like Protagoras, deciding nothing about it)? —In fact, every oath that has been taken both seriously and circumspectly may well have been taken in just this sense. —For if a person is willing simply to swear that God exists, his offer, so it seems, is not to be taken seriously: he may or may not believe it. If there is a God (the deceiver will say), then I have hit the mark: if there is no God, then neither is there anyone to call me to account, and by such an oath I run no risk. —But *if there is a God*, then is there no danger of being caught in a lie deliberately told in order to deceive God himself?

of duties, the problem now is to determine the boundaries of the *science* to which it belongs. Is it to be considered a part of ethics (it is not the right of men in relation to one another that is in question here), or must it be regarded as lying entirely beyond the bounds of pure philosophical morality?

The *formal aspect* of all religion, if religion is defined as "the sum of all duties *as if* (*instar*) they were divine commands," belongs to philosophical morality, in so far as this definition expresses only the relation of reason to the *Idea of God* which reason itself makes. This does not yet make a duty of religion into a duty *to* (*erga*) God, as a Being existing outside our Idea, since in this case we still abstract from His existence. The ground on which man should conceive all his duties in accordance with this *formal* aspect of religion (their relation to a divine will given *a priori*) is only subjectively-logical: that is to say, we cannot very well make obligation (moral necessitation) tangible to ourselves without thereby thinking of *another* person, namely God, and of His will (of which universally legislative reason is only the spokesman). —But this duty *with regard to* God (really with regard to the Idea of such a Being that we make for ourselves) is a duty of man to himself: it is not an objective obligation to fulfill certain services to another person, but only a subjective obligation to strengthen the moral motive in our own legislative reason.

But as for the *material* aspect of religion, the sum of duties *to* (*erga*) God or the service to be rendered Him (*ad praestandum*), this could contain particular duties as divine commands—duties which would not proceed merely from reason giving universal law and which would therefore be known to us only empirically, not *a priori*. Hence these duties would belong only to revealed religion, which would, therefore, also have to presuppose the existence of this Being, not merely the Idea of Him for practical purposes, and to presuppose it, not arbitrarily, but rather as something that could be presented as given immediately or mediately in experience. But such religion still comprises no part of *pure philosophical morality*, no matter what other grounds it might have.

Thus *religion*, as the doctrine of duties *to* God, lies entirely beyond [487] the bounds of pure philosophical ethics, and this fact serves to justify the author of the present [ethical treatise] for not having followed the usual practice of bringing religion, conceived in that sense, into ethics, in order to make it complete.

We can indeed speak of a "religion *within the bounds* of mere reason" which is not, however, derived from mere reason but is based also on the teachings of history and revelation and considers only the *consistency* of pure practical reason with these (that is, shows that there is no conflict between them). But in that case as well religion is not pure: it is rather the doctrine of religion applied to a history handed down to us, and there is no room for it in *ethics*, as pure practical philosophy.

Concluding Note

All the moral relations of rational beings, which comprise a principle of harmony among their wills, can be traced back to *love* and *respect;* and, in so far as this principle is practical, in the case of love the determining ground of the will can be traced back to another's *end*, and in the case of respect, to his *right.* —If one of these beings is such (God) that He has only rights and no duties in relation to the other, so that the other has only duties and no rights in relation to Him, then the principle of the moral relation between them is *transcendent*. On the other hand, the moral relation of men to men, whose wills reciprocally limit one another, has an *immanent* principle.

The divine end with regard to the human race (its creation and direction) can be conceived only as proceeding from *love*—that is, as the *happiness* of men. But the principle of the divine will with regard to the *respect* due to God (honour and fear), which limits the effects of love—that is, the principle of God's right—can be none other than *justice*. To express this in human terms: God has created rational beings from the need, as it were, to have someone outside Himself whom He could love or by whom He could also be loved. [488] But the claim which divine *justice*, and indeed *punitive* justice, makes on us is not only as great but even greater in the judgment of our own reason (because the principle is a limiting one). —For *reward* (*praemium, remuneratio gratuita*) has no place in God's justice to beings who have only duties and no rights in relation to Him, but only in His love and beneficence (*benignitas*) to them; —still less can such beings claim a *requital* (*merces*), and a *justice dispensing such requital* (*iustitia brabeutica*) is a contradiction in the relation of God to men.

But in the Idea of an exercise of justice by a Being Who is above any interference with His ends there is something that cannot well be reconciled with men's relation to God: namely the concept of a *wrong* that could be done to the infinite and inaccessible ruler of the world—for we are not speaking here of men's violations of each other's rights, on which God, as the punishing judge, passes sentence, but of the offense supposed to be done to God Himself and His right. The concept of this is *transcendent*: in other words, it lies entirely beyond the concept of any criminal justice for which we can show any example at all (that is, justice among men) and contains principles that, going beyond all experience, cannot really be brought into accord with those we would use in cases of experience and are, accordingly, quite empty for our practical reason.

Here the Idea of a divine criminal justice is personified; it is not a particular being that exercises this justice as a judge (for then this being would come into contradiction with the principles of Law). Rather, *Justice* —as if it were a substance (otherwise called eternal justice) which, like the *fate* (destiny) of the ancient philosophical poets, is above even Jupiter—announces the law with iron, inevitable necessity, which we cannot penetrate further. Now some examples of this.

Punishment (according to Horace) does not let the criminal out of its sight as he strides proudly before it; rather, it keeps on limping behind him until it catches him. —"Blood innocently shed cries out for vengeance." —"Crime cannot remain unavenged": if the punishment [489] does not strike the criminal, then his descendants must suffer it, or if it does not befall him during his lifetime, then it must take place in a life after death,* which

---

* It is not at all necessary to bring the hypothesis of a future life into this, in order to present that threat of punishment as completely fulfilled. For man, considered as a moral being, will be judged as a supersensible object by a supersensible judge, not under conditions of time: it is only his existence [*Existenz*] that is in question. His life on earth —be it short or long or even eternal—is only its temporal presence [*Dasein*] in appearance, and the concept of justice requires no closer determination. Thus it is not belief in a future life that comes first, in order that we may see the effect of criminal justice in it; on the contrary, it is from the necessity of punishment that the inference to a future life is drawn.

[489]   165

is accepted and readily believed in expressly so that the claim of eternal justice may be satisfied and settled. —"I will not allow *blood-guilt* to come upon my land by granting pardon to an evil, murdering duellist for whom you intercede," a wise ruler once said. —*"Guilt for sins* must be expiated," even if a completely innocent person should have to offer himself as an atonement (in which case the suffering he took upon himself could not properly be called punishment—for he himself had committed no crime); all of which makes it clear that it is not a person administering justice to whom this judgment of condemnation is ascribed (for the person could not speak in this way without doing injustice to the other), but rather that mere *Justice*, as a transcendent principle ascribed to a supersensible subject, determines the right of this being. This right is, indeed, in conformity with the *formal* aspect of this principle, but it is in conflict with the *material* aspect of it—the *end*, which is always the *happiness* of men. For, because of the eventual mass of criminals who keep its record of guilt running on and on, criminal justice would put the *end* of creation, not in the creator's *love* (as we must conceive it to be), but rather in the strict observance of *right* (it would make right itself the end, which is located in the *honour* of God). But since the latter (justice) is only the limiting condition of the former (benevolence), this seems to be in contradiction with [490] principles of practical reason, by which the creator would have had to avoid a creation that could have produced a result so contrary to His intention, which can have only love as its ground.

From all this it is clear that in ethics, as pure practical philosophy of the inner legislation, it is only the moral relations of *men to men* that are intelligible to us. But

the sort of moral relation that holds, in this respect, between God and man surpasses completely the boundaries
of ethics and is altogether inconceivable to us. This, then,
confirms what was maintained above: that ethics cannot go beyond the limits of reciprocal duties of men.

Translator's
Notes to the Text

Page 5, Note 1: Cf. Walter Strauss: *Friedrich Nicolai und die kritische Philosophie;* Stuttgart (1927), p. 23 ff. In 1796 Nicolai, in his *"Beschreibung einer Reise durch Deutschland und die Schweiz im Jahre 1781,"* attacked the use to which Schiller and his followers had put Kantian terminology. Despite Kant's warning that this criticism should not be extended to Critical Philosophy itself, Nicolai did just that with his *"Leben und Meinungen Sempronius Grundiberts"* (1798), which called forth Kant's *"Zwei Briefe an Herrn Friedrich Nicolai."*

Page 6, Note 2: The *Rechtslehre* was first published separately, probably in January 1797. The *Tugendlehre* followed in August of the same year.

Page 36, Note 3: Kant uses the term *Zwang* for compulsion in general, whether it is exercised by other men or by one's own reason. To mark the distinction more clearly I have, for the most part, used "compulsion" for necessitation by other men and "constraint" for necessitation by one's own reason.

Page 42, Note 4: L. Cochius, *Über die Neigungen* (1769)

Page 43, Note 5: Kant's sentence reads: "But because this act . . ." However, this sentence marks the transition from his discussion of action in general to his discussion of moral action in particular.

Page 45, Note 6: *i.e.* "so far as actuality is concerned." The distinction is between actuality and potentiality. In other words, man's striving to raise himself from the crude state

168

of his animality is not directed to his animality as a mere power for realizing ends, or potentiality, but rather to the actuality of these ends in human action.

Page 65, Note 7: "you will travel most safely in the middle of the road"; "too much of anything becomes bad"; "there is a certain measure in our affairs and finally fixed limits, beyond which or short of which one cannot find a good footing" (quoted more fully in Kant's note, page 95); "happy are those who keep to the mean"; "it is a foolish wisdom, equivalent to wickedness, that seeks to be virtuous beyond the proper measure" (also quoted more fully on page 70 and again in Kant's note, page 95). The quotations are from Ovid, *Metamorphoses* II, 137; Horace, *Satires*, I, 1, 105-106; Horace, *Epistles* I, 6, 15.

Page 66, Note 8: In the second edition this section is numbered XIV. Hence the numbers from here on are one less than in the second edition.

Page 72, Note 9: The sense of this sentence seems to require a transposing of Kant's phrase "(lawfulness from purposefulness)."

Page 74, Note 10: In view of Kant's later explanation (page 147), the second edition emends the preceding sentence to read: "the method of the first exercise (in the theory of duties) is called *didactic*, and here the manner of teaching is either *lecturing* or *questioning*. The latter is the art of asking the pupil what he already knows about concepts of duty."

Page 74, Note 11: The first edition has "Catechetic." Cf. page 73, note 10.

Page 76, Note 12: The first edition, again, reads "Catechetic."

Page 82, Note 13: In view of Kant's explanation on page 88, the second edition changes the preceding passage to read: "c) the preservation of the subject's ability to use his powers purposefully and to enjoy," etc.

Page 86, Note 14: *i.e.* Frederick the Great.

Page 88, Note 15: *i.e.* as the form of the deed in so far as it carries guilt with it. The *species facti* is the totality of those characteristics of the deed which pertain essentially to its imputability. Cf. Baumgarten, *Initia philosophiae practicae*, 128 (*Akademie* ed., vol. xix, p. 62)

Page 91, Note 16: *i.e.* "his valor is enkindled by wine." Horace, Odes, III, 21, 11.

Page 91, Note 17: In the first edition the sentence "But who can determine . . . for measuring" follows the sentence "The use of opium . . . only as medicines."

Page 92, Note 18: The saying actually occurs in Gellius, *Noctes Atticae*, XIII, 11.

Page 92, Note 19: *i.e.* "to have one thing ready on the tongue and another shut up in the heart." Sallust Catil., 10

Page 96, Note 20: In place of the passage: "nor, again, do I mean . . . that I am referring to here" the second edition has: "I mean, rather, *miserly avarice*, which is called stinginess or niggardliness when it is shameful; and I am concerned with this kind of avarice, not in so far as it consists in mere neglect of one's duties of love to others, but in so far as it is a restricting of *one's own* use of the means to good living so narrowly as to leave one's true needs unsatisfied and is thus contrary to one's duty *to oneself*." In fact, only two kinds of avarice—prodigality and miserliness—are in question.

Page 97, Note 21: The second edition omits "and keep" in the preceding sentence.

Page 103, Note 22: *i.e.*, "These trifles lead to serious things."

Page 114, Note 23: Following the second edition. The first edition also leaves open the possibility: "(though, because of that weakness, virtues are not commonly called vice)." The resolution to practice virtue must be made all at once and as a whole, but the "frailty of human nature" means that there will be lapses in putting the resolution into practice.

Page 116, Note 24: Haller, *Über die Ewigkeit* (1736)

NOTES

Page 138, Note 25: In place of the passage: "and to reverence the law ... due him (*observantia debita*)," the second edition has: "and to observe the law also with regard to other men ... due him (*observantia debita*)."

Page 139, Note 26: In the following paragraphs 45 to 48, I have found Professor Paton's analysis and translation of the material most helpful. Cf. H. J. Paton: "Kant on Friendship," *Proceedings of the British Academy, Volume* XLII, pp. 45-66.

Page 144, Note 27: *i.e.* "a bird that is rare on earth, quite like a black swan." Juvenal, *Satires* II, 6, 165.

Page 161, Note 28: The reference is actually to Cicero, *De natura deorum*, I, 23, 63.

Index

aesthetic, of morals, 68; predispositions to morality, 59 ff.
agitations (*Affekten*), 69 ff., 143
ambition, *see* pride
amphiboly of moral concepts of reflection, 108 ff.
animality in man, 12, 36, 82-83, 84 ff.; *see also* humanity
anthropology, 44, 67; moral, 14
antinomy of duties to oneself, 79 ff.
apathy, moral, 69-71
appetitive power, 7, 9
ascetic, moral, 74 ff., 158 ff.
autonomy of practical reason, 41, 152
avarice, 65, 96 ff., 120

benevolence, *see* love, duties of

calumny, 136 ff.
casuistry, 73-74, 75, 157-158
catechism, 74n., 75n., 150 ff.
choice (*Willkür*), 9 ff., 11; free and animal, 10, 26; distinct from *Wille* 10, 25 ff., 69; matter and form of, 31, 33, 38 ff.; *see also* ends
concupiscence, 9
conflict of duties, 23
conscience, 54, 60 ff., 103 ff.
contempt, 107, 132 ff.
constraint, 62, 66; external (compulsion) 18, 40-41; and self-constraint, 36-39, 40-41, 54-57; *see also* necessitation, legislation
contentment with oneself, 34, 46-47, 50-51
cultivation of one's powers, 45-46, 51 ff., 82, 110 ff., 120, 157 ff.; *see also* perfection

deed, 22, 103
disposition to the good, 107-108, 134, 157
duty, defined, 21, 123, 155; divisions of, 75, 81 ff., 115 ff.; into directly and indirectly ethical, 17-18; narrow and wide, 49-50, 51 ff., 72 ff., 97n., 112 ff., 117; negative and positive, 81-82; juridical, 11, 17, 40-41, 48-49, 54-55, 117, 126; of virtue, 38-39, 54 ff., 57-58, 72-73, 81 ff., 117

ends, defined, 38, 43; and means, 38 ff., 48-49; as matter of law, 33, 48; man as end in himself, 55-56, 85, 94, 97, 99, 117, 132; subjective and objective, 38 ff., 47, 48-49; *see also* duty of virtue
enthusiasm, 71
envy, 127-129
ethics, defined, 36, 39, 72; distinct from Law, 31, 36, 68, 92; divisions of, 71 ff., 139-140; first principle of, 55 ff.; limits of, 139-140, 161 ff.
examples, good and bad, 152

fantastic virtue, 71, 98
feeling, 7 ff., 32 ff.; moral, 46, 59 ff.; *see also* pleasure
final end, 31n., 67, 107
frailty of human nature, 113
freedom, 10 ff., 19 ff., 22, 25 ff., 35; and nature, 11 ff., 43 ff., 111; inner, 54-55, 66, 69, 80-81, 83; outer, 38, 56; inner and outer, 11, 38, 56-57, 68; *see also* laws
friendship 140 ff.

gratitude, 109, 123-124, 127, 128-129

172

INDEX

greed, 97

God, Idea of, *see* religion

habit, 41-42, 71-72

happiness, and moral laws, 12 ff., 34-35, 154 ff.; as divine end, 164 ff.; of others, 46 ff., 53 ff., 58, 117 ff.; one's own, 46 ff., 120

hatred, vices of, 127 ff.

health, moral, 42, 71, 82, 159

holiness, 36, 57, 113 ff.

humanity, and man, 37n., 45-46, 67, 80, 82-83, 85-86, 92 ff., 107-108, 110-111, 118-119, 132; and animality, 45-46, 51, 60; right of, 50, 122

humility, 100 ff.

hypocrisy, 101, 158

imperatives, and maxims, 10-11, 24, 25; and ends, 43 ff., 48, 55-57, *see also* ends; and laws, *see* laws; categorical, 24, 40, and conditioned, 20, 43, 46

imputation, 27-28, 103 ff.

inclination, 9, 10, 17, 37n., 54, 71, 120, 149, 152, 154, 156

ingratitude, *see* gratitude

instincts, 82-83

intemperance, 90 ff.

interest, 9, 56, 138, 158

judgment, 133, 150; moral, 27, 73 ff., 103 ff.

latitude, *see* duty, wide

Law, 1-2, 38, 40, 50, 56-57, 72, 92; *see also* right

laws of freedom defined, 27; and imperatives, 19-20, 20-21, 36-37; and laws of nature, 11 ff., 15, 43, 111; natural and positive, 23-24; contingent, 27; juridical and ethical, 12, 40, 56 ff.; permissive, 22, 89

legality of actions, 11, 17, 25, 53, 58

legislation, 14, 16 ff., 23, 48 ff., 53-54, 118-119; ethical and juridical, 16 ff.; inner and outer, 17-18, 27, 35, 72

legislator, 27; authority of, 24

love, 62-63, 72, 89-90, 115-117, 145; divine, 164 ff.; duties of, 117 ff., 163; in friendship, 140 ff.

lying, 64, 83, 92-96, 155

malicious joy, 129-130

mathematics, 4-5, 64

merit, meritorious, 27, 50-51, 115

metaphysics defined, 2, 14, 31; of morals, 11, 14 ff., 33

metaphysical first principles, of doctrine of Law, 1 ff., 31; of doctrine of virtue, 1 ff., 32 ff., 139-140, 161 ff.; of natural science, 1 ff., 11, 14

mockery, 137-138

moderation, 131-132

moral feeling, *see* feeling

morality of actions, 11, 17, 41, 52, 58

moral laws, *see* laws

morally indifferent actions, 21-22, 71; *see also* permissible

moral worth, lack of, 42, 49, 69, 114, 134

motive, law as, 32 ff., 41, 50, 52, 58, 113 ff., 152

nature's purposes, 82-83, 87 ff., 93

necessitation, moral, 20-21, 25-26, 44, 59-60, 79, 103, 108, 120, 123, 162

obligation, defined, 18-19, 20 ff., 40-41, 59-60, 140; subjects of, 75, 79 ff., 108 ff., 115, 123 ff.

obsessions (*Leidenschaften*), 69 ff.

perfection, 44 ff., 66-67, 107, 113-114; *see also* cultivation

permissible actions, 20, 21, 134; *see also* laws, permissive